Dear Saver,

We'd like to take this opportunity to personally thank you for visiting one of American Savings' many offices for your copy of GREAT OLDTIME RECIPES. This new cookbook takes a refreshing look at the exciting world of preparing natural foods in an easy, old-fashioned manner with savory results.

Before you read through these delicious, nutritious descriptions including recipes published as early as 1727, take a look at why so many Californians choose American for all their savings needs:

Over 90 convenient locations
High interest on insured savings
A full range of savings plans
Many free saver services available to account holders
Postage paid save-by-mail service
Keogh/IRA tax-deferred retirement plans

These, plus our friendly people, and the extra protection of insured safety for your savings are combined to make American Savings one of the nation's largest financial institutions.

Sincerely,

William J. Popejoy
President

S. Mark Taper
Chairman of the Board

AMERICAN SAVINGS AND LOAN ASSOCIATION
Safe since 1885

Great
Oldtime
Recipes

Beatriz-Maria Prada

BALLANTINE BOOKS • NEW YORK

Library of Congress Catalog Card Number: 74-6243

ISBN 0-345-28018-0

Cover photo by Laszlo

Manufactured in the United States of America

First Ballantine Books Edition: June 1974
Second Special Printing: January 1980

For two great people:
my aunt, Maria Prada,
and my father, Pedro Luis Prada

My thanks go to the Rare Book Division, the New York Public Library, Astor, Lenox, and Tilden Foundations, for permission to use material from:

American Cookery, by Amelia Simmons (facsimile, published by the Oxford University Press, 1958);

The Book of Household Management, by Mrs. Isabella Beeton (first edition, 1861);

The Indian Meal Book, by Eliza Leslie (first edition, 1846).

❧

My special thanks also go to Edward Callahan, Toni Huberman, and Pamela McGhan, who helped with the research; to Magi English, my editorial assistant, whose enthusiasm was unflagging; to the Bazar Français, for information on old and new kitchen equipment; to the Integral Yoga Institute; and finally, to my son Peter, who always rises to the occasion, whatever it may be.

Contents

Introduction   xv

1 ABOUT THOSE GREAT, OLDTIME
  COOKS AND THEIR RECIPES   1

    Cooks as Artists; Cooking in America;
    Eliza Smith, First Cookbook Writer Pub-
    lished in this Country; Amelia Simmons,
    First All-American Cookbook Author; Nine-
    teenth-century Cookbook Authors; What
    We Can Glean about Them; How to Use
    the Recipes; Old Versus New Equipment;
    Using the Oven Temperature Chart; Old-
    time Cookware; The Safest Cookware

2 SOUPS, SAUCES, AND TASTY MORSELS
                                           17

    Vegetable Soups, including Pea, Irish Po-
    tato, and Herb with Parmesan, Shrimp
    Gumbo, Bean Soups, Nut Soups, including
    Almond Milk, Queen Victoria's Own Soup,
    Cereal and Fruit Soups; Beer Soup
    Francatelli on sauce-making; Basic Sauces,
    including Tomato, Economical White Sauce,
    and Melted Butter; Shellfish Sauces, Arrow-

root, and Gooseberry Sauces; Dumplings, Croutons, and Egg Balls

3 *HEARTY DISHES WITH CHICKEN, TUR-
   KEY, AND FISH*   55

How to Choose Poultry; Chicken Burdwan; Pressed and Breakfast Chicken; Boudins; Croquettes

Roast Turkey with Gravy and Oyster Stuffing; Turkey Scallop; Turkey Legs with
Chestnut Puree

About Fish; Boiled and Baked Fish with
Stuffing; Chowder; Devilled Clams and
Crabs; Cooking Fish in Clay; Codfish Dishes,
including Codfish with Walnuts; Oyster
Shortcake; Fillets of Salmon a l'Indienne;
Sardine Sauté; Scallop Dishes; Broiled Span-
ish Mackeral; Sole Pie; Devilled Whitebait

4 *LIGHTER DISHES WITH EGGS AND
   CHEESE, AND SOME WITH BEANS AND
   RICE*   97

About Barnyard Hens and Their Eggs;
How to Make a Soufflé, Boiled Eggs and
Other Hints on Cooking Eggs; Egg Cutlets
and Creamed Eggs; Omelets, including Fine
Herbs and Rum; Curried Eggs; Egg and
Bread Dishes

How to make Cheese; Toasted Cheese;
Canapes; Welsh Rarebits; Cayenne Cheese
Straws; Fondue and Soufflé; Baked Eggs
and Cheese; Sandwiches

Bean Porridge; Lima Beans; Nutritional
Content of White versus Brown Rice; Jam-
balaya of Fowls and Rice; Eggs on Rice;
Omelet and Turkish Croquettes

5   *VEGETABLES AND SALADS—GOD'S GIFT
    TO THE UNIVERSE*   137

How to Bake Eliza Smith's Cabbage-Lettuce Pye; Asparagus with Eggs; Corn Pudding; Eggplant Stuffed with Nuts; Mushrooms on Toast; Peas in Potato Cases;
Stuffed Peppers; About Potatoes: Baked and
Broiled Potatoes; Potato Pancake; Sweet
Potatoes; Vegetable Curry

Poet's Recipe for Salad; Washing Vegetables; Celery Salad; Dandelion Salad; English Salads; Lettuce Lemon Salad; Mint
Lemon Salad; Lettuce Salad with Egg Dressing; Japanese Salad; Potato Salad and Salad
Dressing

6   *OLDFASHIONED PIES, PUDDINGS, AND
    OTHER SWEET GOODIES*   161

How to Make Eliza Smith's Carrot Pud-
ding (Pie); How to Make Pastry; Apple
Pies, including Apple Custard Pie; Grape
Pie; Mock Mince Pie; Dried Peach Custard
Pie; Pumpkin Pie; Pie á la Martha Wash-
ington; Hazelnut Tarts; Shortcakes

How to Steam, Boil, and Bake Puddings;
Half Hour Pudding; Apple Puddings;
Quick Puddings; Boiled Rice Pudding; Fig
Rice Pudding; Tapioca Pudding; Pudding á
la Zouave; Christmas Plum Puddings; Car-
rot Pudding

How to Make Custards: Orange, Straw-
berry, Cocoanut, Almond; How to Serve
Fruits: Strawberries, Cantaloupe, Currants;
Huckleberries with Crackers and Cream;

Huckleberry Shortcake; About Fools and Flummeries; Apricot Fool; Strawberry Flummery; Potato Rolls; Orange Sponge

7 REALLY GREAT, OLDFASHIONED ICE CREAM   205

About Ice Cream; How to Use a Freezing Machine; Types of Ice Cream; Vanilla Ice Cream; Ice Cream Made with Arrowroot; Pure Ice Cream: Chocolate, Cocoanut and Fruit Cream; Fruit Ice Cream; Brown Bread Ice Cream; Other Delicious Flavors, including Plum Pudding; Lemon, Pineapple, and Raspberry Sherberts

8 CAKES AND COOKIES, BREADS AND DROPCAKES, AND SOME OLDTIME FRITTERS   223

How to Bake an Oldfashioned Cake; How to Bake Eliza Smith's Ordinary Cake; Croquante Cake; Seed Cake; Rice Cake; Love Cake; Hickory Cake; Berry Cake; Cider Cake; Wedding Cake: How to Make; Plum Cake; Pound Cake; How to Make a Tiered Cake; Almond Paste; Fudge and Cream Cheese Frostings; Crisp Cookies; Trifles; Hermits; Ginger-Snaps; Cocoanut Cookies; New York Cookies

How to Bake Bread; Entire or Wholewheat Bread; Pulled Bread; Buttered Toast; Rice Waffles; Rye, Oatmeal, Corn Dropcakes; French Fritter Batter; Fruit Fritters; Apple Fritters; Clam Fritters; Chicken Fritters

9 *CURRY POWDERS, POTTED SPREADS, AND OTHER ODDMENTS; WINES AND A POTPOURRI OF BEAUTY NOSTRUMS* 257

About Oldtime Household Hints and Remedies; Aromatic Herbaceous Seasoning; Indian Chutney; Curry Powders; · Potted Fish; Nut Butter; Orange Butter; Strawberry Jam; Grape Jelly; Currant Wine; Raspberry Wine; Champagne Cup; Vegetarian Coffee; Molasses Candy; Chocolate Kisses; Candied Fruit; Candied Pumpkin; Cookery for the Poor; How to Make Potpourri, Scent Powder, Lavender Bags; How to Make the Complexion Soft and Fine; Sarah Bernhardt's Beauty Secrets; How to Press Plants

USEFUL INFORMATION 279

Oldtime Hints for Saving Fuel—and Dollars

Recipes Using Only Egg Yolks or Egg Whites

Oven Temperature Chart

Some Useful Measures

List of Antique Cookbooks and Writers

INDEX 289

*Great
Oldtime
Recipes*

Introduction

Dear Reader:

Writing about these oldtime cookbook authors and their recipes—worked out so carefully in an age when housewifery was indeed an art—I felt I'd stretched my hand across the years and touched the souls of artists still very much alive.

I got to know these delightful personalities from the past quite intimately—how they lived and what they thought about food and other important matters, their experiences of lives so much the same yet so different from ours today.

Eliza Smith, Amelia Simmons, Charles Elmé Francatelli, to name but three—they all produced works of art, lovingly assembled, printed, and bound for you and me to use, as other readers did so long ago.

I can easily imagine the eager young homemaker (bustling about a copper-hung kitchen, a dimity apron covering her huge hooped skirt of sprigged silk) whose busy fingers first caressed the pages of my 1730 copy of Eliza Smith's *The Compleat Housewife*, softening the leather cover to its smooth patina. And I can see clearly the serious, Victorian housewife, noting in her spiky, old-fashioned script a treasured cheesecake recipe on a scrap of paper and placing it for safety between the pages of Miss Shute's *The American Housewife*—where I found it nearly a century later.

And the recipes created by these inspired, oldtime cooks? Absolutely great; so good in fact that it broke my heart to leave out those that ran beyond the space allotted.

So, with thanks to those wonderful, old-world housewife-cooks, and to the great epicurean chefs of America's banqueting years—let's all enjoy

Good cooking and good eating,

BEATRIZ-MARIA PRADA

January, 1974

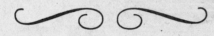

I

About Those Great, Oldtime Cooks and Their Recipes

"Now and then some inspired being arises capable of demonstrating the wonderful pitch of excellence to which cookery may be carried." So wrote Miss T. S. Shute back in 1879. She could have been speaking of herself—but unwittingly, for she was a cultured and modest person.

All the same, if you're a typical cook of today, coping with domestic problems Miss Shute never dreamed of, a comment like hers bangs against the old brain cells. For most of us are not geniuses (rare birds that crop up once or twice in a lifetime), but we do claim to be artists at the stove. And artists emphatically root for the unusual, the inspired—and the antique, for the latter has an ambiance missing from its modern counterpart.

Antique recipes have ambiance in full measure, something that's impossible to get from, say, a new-style blender recipe sure to go right because it's machine-made. (And I'm not knocking blenders—I use mine often, for recipes old and new.)

But the fact is that when Miss Shute tells me "vegetables should be carefully cleaned from insects, and nicely washed," I'm hooked—inspired to grow my own, if only in a window-box, just so I can catch God's smallest creatures ducking in and out of the dark spinach leaves I'm at pains to wash nicely.

And that word "nicely"—it defies definition, yet I know exactly what Miss Shute means.

Then the ingredients listed in antique recipes (except for some like orange-flower water and rose essence, which were forgotten until recently) are mostly tried-and-true favorites. Yet the housewife-chef of days gone by combined them with nuances we've lost or forgotten: for instance, Mrs. Rundell's Orange

Butter, a mouthwatering concoction of hard-boiled eggs, orange-flower water, and almond paste.

The recipes in the pages that follow appear in cookbooks printed during the period from 1727 to 1908; and thereby hangs a tale. For as we eat, so we are, and so we live; and the whole picture is laid out right there by the author-cooks.

Eliza Smith's colossal "pyes," for instance, weren't a bite too big for her hungry family, which no doubt comprised not only relatives, but a houseful of servants, both male and female, as well as a herd of poor relations—elderly aunts and uncles, and perhaps an unfortunate girl-cousin or two without dowry or husband and thus homeless, who'd be pushed about by family and servants alike.

All these people had to be fed; in addition, both America and England of Eliza's day were rural—and, as anyone who's lived on a farm (as I have) will tell you, farmhands have huge appetites. After all this, Eliza's pies surely shrink to normal size.

Happily (or unhappily?) for the housewife, by the latter part of the nineteenth century the family had shed many members, and most had ceased to be rural. Mrs. Henderson, for instance, was no farmer's wife but a woman of urban social standing. By her time (the 1870s), therefore, recipe quantities were decidedly smaller, with cooks creating everyday dishes for six rather than twenty people.

Finally, in 1909, a cookbook came out called *Cooking for Two*, a title Eliza Smith would have laughed at merrily.

Colonial housewives worked out their own recipes—which they guarded jealously against neighborly theft—without expert aid even from their British cousins, one or two of whom had already published cookbooks.

Then, in 1742, William Parks, a publisher from Williamsburg, Virginia, took a chance on one of these engaging little books—Eliza Smith's *The Compleat Housewife or Accomplish'd Gentlewoman's Compan-*

ion. It was a success in England from the day it first came out in 1727; by 1730 it had gone into its fourth edition (of which I'm proud to own a copy). Mr. Parks's hunch paid off: Eliza's book was snapped up by colonial housewives hungry for cookery knowhow in printed form.

Thus the great spate of cookbooks started, first as an interchange between English and American authors, then as an unprecedented flow of millions of books, on both sides of the Atlantic. The end of the nineteenth century saw enough cookbooks published to satisfy all but the most discriminating collector.

Nevertheless, despite the excellence of Eliza Smith's recipes, a few of which you can evaluate yourself in these pages, American housewives hankered after recipes for such yummy local dishes as Indian Meal Pudding and Sweet Potato Pie—all mysterious, unknown foodstuffs to those English housewives who authored the early cookbooks, and thus missing from their pages.

In true Horatio Alger style, however, it was "An American Orphan"—as Amelia Simmons describes herself—who in 1796 repaired this annoying omission, thus becoming the first all-American cookbook author.

A born writer though almost illiterate, Amelia produced with much sweat of brow and brain a remarkable little book of forty-eight pages, written in clearcut language and presented with a naïve charm. In *American Cookery,* Amelia included such dishes as Apple Pie and Indian Pudding, giving the book an essentially American touch despite the English culinary principles she obviously cooked by. Inexpensively bound (Amelia even picked up the printing tab) and priced at two shillings and threepence, the book deservedly ran into several editions, the sales of which must have nicely augmented the little orphan's nest egg.

During the early 1800s, although Amelia Simmons's work had many imitators (and one outright plagiarism), it was Mrs. Mary Eliza Ketelby Rundell's *A New System of Domestic Cookery* (published in England in 1806, and in America in 1821 as *The Experienced American Housekeeper*) which topped the as-yet-unrecorded bestseller lists.

British Mrs. Rundell apologizes for the simplicity of her recipes which, she explains, she'd written for her married daughters, not for "professed cooks." As she goes on to say, with pardonable lack of modesty, "This little work would have been a treasure to herself when she first set out in life." Her book went into many editions, challenged only later by compatriot Mrs. Isabella Beeton's colossal *Book of Household Management*.

Then into the cookery lists came America's Eliza Leslie, a writer of "tales" who produced recipe books regularly through the thirties and forties. A traveled gentlewoman who'd certainly visited England and possibly France, Eliza nevertheless rooted for American food, Southern cooking—and its superb exponent, the Negro cook.

Running to 1112 pages, Mrs. Beeton's *The Book of Household Management* (1861) was the first of those tomes in which every detail you can think of about cooking and household management is listed, described, and annotated; even the quantities in Mrs. Beeton's recipes are small, modern style.

In addition to her matter-of-fact recipes, Mrs. Beeton comes up with rare tidbits: how to boil—she must've meant beat—an egg, Oriental fashion, by swinging it around your head in a cloth (the luckless thing practically curdles); and whether or not you can marry your second cousin (in Victorian England, yes, according to Mrs. B.). A handy book indeed.

In pathetic contrast, two years later (1863), a little volume of a handful of pages, its original cover printed on wallpaper, attested to the terrible hardships suffered by the Confederate South during the Civil War. Squeezed to starving point by Lincoln's blockade, the rebelling states were in urgent need of food. *The Confederate Receipt Book,* published by West and Johnston of Richmond, Virginia, features one recipe "adapted to the times"—Apple Pie without Apples (soak, presumably in water, one small bowl of crackers, together with 1 teaspoonful of tartaric acid, butter, and a little nutmeg; sweeten to taste). Incidentally, only five copies of this incredible book are known to exist.

By 1835, cookbook writing had become a fact of publishing life in both America and Europe. In France, the two great chefs, Jean Anthelme Brillat-Savarin and Carême had taken up the pen, while in England during the same period Alexis Soyer had adapted his *haute cuisine* to the housewife's talents, as Francatelli was to do so delightfully decades later.

During the same period, poetess Eliza (what magic's in that name?) Acton gleaned a bigger fortune with her cookbooks on both sides of the Atlantic than through the poetry for which she was also famous.

Undoubtedly, the most famous total vegetarian of the nineteenth century was another, far greater, poet, Percy Bysshe Shelley, whose diet of vegetables only, with no protein, was guaranteed to land him eventually in the nuthouse (Shelley was known to be neurotic). The members of the Vegetarian Society of the same period were wiser. They followed diets similar to that featured by William Alexander Alcott in the 1849 edition of his *Vegetable Diet,* which the good gentlemen sponsored. Vegetarian Alcott gives recipes for omelets, macaroni, and oatmeal, as well as for vegetables—the essence of an all-around, natural-foods diet today.

Such a diet is proposed by Dr. Dio Lewis, a delightful personality straight out of Dickens. His book, *Our Digestion; or, My Jolly Friend's Secret,* published later, in 1872, is one of several written in this vein following an incredible event in medical history.

On June 6, 1822, the innards of a French-Canadian, Alexis St. Martin, were jagged open by an accidental musket shot into a two-and-a-half-inch hole revealing the gastric workings of his stomach to all viewers, including his physician, Dr. William Beaumont. Thereafter, Alexis's life became a paranoidal hell, for Dr. Beaumont, realizing his good fortune in having a living X-ray plate for a patient, mercilessly pursued the luckless victim in quest of the medical knowledge only he could reveal.

It was a timely event; people had already become interested in vegetarianism, in nutrition, and now in health. Books on these subjects proliferated; but Dr. Lewis's beats them all in its light-hearted yet basically sound approach.

After 1850, competition among cookbook writers became rife, cosmopolitan—and scrambling. Even Mrs. Charles Dickens, writing aristocratically under the pseudonym, Lady Maria Clutterbuck, strove to outstrip her famous husband with *What Shall We Have for Dinner?* (guess who won that race), while under the theatrical name of Christopher Crowfield, Harriet Beecher Stowe came up with *House and Home Papers* in 1865. Through the fifties and sixties, *Peterson's Magazine* regularly featured a recipe column; the more literary *Godey's* and *Graham's,* however, did not.

But it is the ladylike Miss T. S. Shute, author of *The American Housewife,* published in 1879, who emerges as the culinary heroine of her era, for her book was sponsored by a baking-powder company. So what? Plenty—saleratus (baking soda to you, and the main ingredient in baking powder) was regarded by many housewives of the period as near-poison. Miss Shute's book obviously did much to allay their fears.

In 1887, Hugo Ziemann, White House chef to Grover Cleveland, and Mrs. F. L. Gillette produced the *White House Cook Book,* which suffers from another first, or near first. Their publisher used cheap newspaper stock instead of the rag paper that makes the earlier cookbooks such sturdy volumes—so every time I open my copy, chippings of yellowed paper shower the floor.

On the other hand, Charles Elmé Francatelli (*haute cuisine* chef to Queen Victoria) was luckier in his choice of publisher: his *Cook's Guide* (a simplified version of his *Modern Cook*) is beautifully printed and bound, with finely engraved illustrations—as befits the creative genius of the great chef whose picture adorns the frontispiece.

Alessandro Filippini (like Charles Ranhofer, one of Delmonico's great chefs) whose book *The Table* antedates Ranhofer's *The Epicurean* by a few years, modestly refrains from publishing his picture. But his recipes speak for themselves—clearly explained, with even the most complicated made easy to follow; not a step is omitted or glossed over. Like his Italian compatriot Francatelli, this man knew his stuff and did not hesitate to pass on his knowledge.

A first-rate compiler (but not a chef), Lafcadio Hearn was a newspaperman with superb culinary taste. His *La Cuisine Créole*, first published in 1885, was a bestselling favorite which continued to find readers well into the twentieth century.

Several of the most famous American cookbooks of the nineteenth century were written by principals of then-thriving cookery schools. Maria Parloa heads a distinguished list which includes Mrs. D. A. Lincoln, who led the Boston Cookery School made so famous later by Fannie Farmer.

Marion Harland (pseudonym of Mary Virginia Hawes Terhune, principal of the National School) teamed up with (presumably) her sister-in-law, Christine Terhune Herrick, to edit a five-volume set called the *Consolidated Library of Modern Cooking and Household Recipes*. This all-encompassing series —the authors devote one volume solely to etiquette—

takes in recipes by "a list of contributors which includes many of the famous chefs and cooking experts
of the United States"—unfortunately anonymous except for Oscar of the Waldorf.

By 1900, no housekeeping magazine was complete
without such directions as how to grace a leg of mut-
ton with a modest paper frill. Newspapers featured
recipes routinely, and if Emma Paddock Telford's
The Evening Telegram Cook Book is typical, these
were well worked out and easy to follow.

In 1901, twin volumes the size of small prayerbooks,
titled respectively *365 Breakfast Dishes* and *365 Desserts*, came out presenting many local talents, including Marion Harland's, Mrs. Lincoln's, and some originally published in a Philadelphia periodical called
Table Talk. The lady editors featured only simple but
tasty recipes, easy to fix—already the servant problem
was on the horizon.

Actually, we know little about the "inspired beings,"
as Miss Shute calls the great culinary artists whose
recipes appear in these pages, except what we can
glean from their writings. But we do know, for instance, that Eliza Smith was a fashion-conscious
woman of mature years, for she mentions with pride
thirty years of cooking prowess. And she also tells us,
"It has grown as unfashionable for a book to appear in
public without a preface, as for a lady to appear without a hoop-skirt," not foreseeing that only three years
later—by 1730, the date of the fourth edition of her
book—the hooped skirt would be as dead as only an
outmoded style can be.

Nevertheless, the hooped skirt had enjoyed a good
innings, and one can imagine Eliza bustling about
cooking, negotiating its enormous width which was
graded to the hemline—in fact, it was so wide at this
point that those giant stairways characteristic of
English houses of this period were built to accom-
modate milady's intransigent skirt.

On the other hand, the slim Amelia Simmons—she

eschews cream in favor of milk—in 1796 wore no hooped skirt; as a probably poor relation, she dressed quietly, in a skirt made full with petticoats, worn below a cross-over bodice which would be sashed.

We can easily visualize the social standing of Mrs. Maria Eliza Ketelby Rundell—the first part of her book gives those married daughters instructions on preparing the table according to their station in life. One can imagine this grande dame of the early 1800s a little passé in her dress (in those days garments, like the works of art they are, were hoarded for decades), wearing a high, beribboned lace cap above a tight bodice and full skirt, a soft black fichu-shawl of lace draped about her shoulders—the mark of the matron.

In contrast, her attentive daughters might be wearing the new French style of the Directoire, within a year or so to become that big bonnetted English fashion shown in Kate Greenaway's charming illustrations.

Sad to relate, the lovely Mrs. Isabella Beeton (she was a great beauty)—collecting material for her cookbook dressed in the latest in morning outfits, crinolined and with softly caped shoulder line and full sleeves—was not to live to enjoy her success. Five years after her book came out, Mrs. Beeton passed away at twenty-nine, leaving her publisher-husband, Samuel, heartbroken and distraught.

Mrs. Mary F. Henderson (*Practical Cooking, and Dinner Giving*, 1876), on the other hand, lived to a good age—or so we can assume from the commanding manner of her treatment of servants, and indirectly, her reader. In her dark, bustled day dress with its high neckline, and her tight forehead curls, she no doubt looked stern and perhaps a little forbidding.

The picture of Francatelli engraved on the frontispiece of his *Cook's Guide* shows a handsome man sporting a fine moustache, a half-smile about his generous mouth. He is a charming, good-looking old boy, with the air of an oldtime actor. He readily forgives his young feminine readers their silly mistakes, for clearly he loves them all.

By the early 1890s, few women could bend, breathe easily, run or move their midriffs, for this was the age of the clinching corset. Those housewife-chefs who compiled such delicious recipes in *365 Breakfast Dishes* and *365 Desserts* were forced to keep their bodies in a permanent upright position—that is, until they released their stays, flopping out exhausted in the privacy of their bedrooms. Fortunately, the masochistic style by this time had reached its peak— tighter lacing would have chopped these ladies in two —and in an incredibly short space of time, actually little over a decade—milady's waist was unlaced and uncorseted in freedom symbolic of the new age. And if she wasn't consulting *Cooking for Two,* she was delving into Dr. Lulu Peters's *Diet and Health* for hints on how to lose weight.

How to Use the Recipes

YOU'LL find the recipes created by these redoubtable cooks sparkle with good ideas you can easily adapt to natural-foods cooking.

Actually, oldtime cooks used mostly natural foods, except for cereals, which unfortunately were milled "white" almost totally by 1850. White sugar of course was used extensively by the end of the nineteenth century, when housewives wielded the forcing bag over almost every cake and dessert.

I selected therefore only those recipes which are basically "natural-foods" style. Thus, all are easy to make, and you'll find no gargantuan, rich-thick dishes impossible to cope with. Alternative natural-foods ingredients are given with some recipes, while the protein emphasis is on fish, poultry, eggs, and cheese, with no meat in the running—in company with many people, I find meat too acid, and for this reason never put it on the menu.

You'll find the proper grind of wholegrain flour indicated in each recipe. The difference in time (one hour versus twenty minutes) in cooking wholegrain rice in place of white is also noted.

Also indicated is the shorter time used to conserve nutrients when cooking fruits and vegetables.

Like salt, the amount of sugar used in any recipe varies with personal taste. Turbinado has less sweetening power than white sugar, so that when you substitute the former you automatically reduce the oversweetening by oldtime cooks with extra-sweet tooths.

Quantities are mostly for six or eight, which can save the headache of doubling the usual recipe for four; on the other hand, to serve two or four, you face the problem of how to reduce the amounts without affecting the recipe. Your best bet is to cook the full recipe; then either freeze extras, eat them cold the next day, or give them away to a neighbor. If you do halve or quarter the amounts, you may feel like reworking the recipe—subtleties tend to get lost in the changeover, particularly when the recipe has several ingredients.

Oldtime Equipment versus Modern

IF you're wondering whether the recipes will work if cooked in modern utensils, the answer is yes—most kitchen equipment has changed little through the centuries.

Oldtime cooks used saucepans, griddles, frying pans, choppers, and even gadgets such as melon scoops as we do today. The only basic difference (except for electrifying) is that the oldies are far better made—knife blades (of unchromed steel) are sharper, wooden handles stouter and firmer than plastic; while gadgets come solidly produced in thick, hard metal. Even the early electrical appliances are more solidly constructed. In fact, many cooks (myself included) prefer working with old equipment.

Updating the Oldtime Stove with the Oven Temperature Chart

THE Oven Temperature Chart at the back of the book will show you at what temperature to set your modern oven for cooking bread, cakes, etc.; it also gives the equivalent temperature in degrees for the directions "moderate," "hot," and so forth.

The one piece of equipment that's changed radically through the years is the stove, and to understand phrases such as "back of the stove" which appear often in oldtime recipes, you'll need to know how those ancient wood-burning wonders worked.

The oldtime stove was constructed of cast iron, and shaped in the form of a giant box. The fire burned in the center, with the smoke rising out of the chimney in the rear. The top of the "box" was punctured with holes acting as burners, over which cooks placed their pots, and through which you could see the red-hot, and sometimes flaming, fire roaring away below. If you got too close, though, you'd scorch your face, so intense was the heat that surged up.

Bringing down the heat to moderate, however, was an easy matter; you merely closed up the hell-like aperture with a special lid that fitted flush so you could stand your pot upon it.

On baking day, the oldtime housewife would fill the oven section with breads and cakes all placed in positions according to the degree of heat needed to cook them. She could reduce the temperature also by leaving the door open—all of which makes us marvel at her skill, which incidentally is by no means lost. I know cooks—and you may, too—who've mastered the art of cooking on an oldtime wood-burning stove. Their verdict's unanimous—in many respects that antique stove is a far better design than its modern counterpart.

Oldtime Cookware—Modern Standby

IN essentials, oldtime cookware differs little from that of today. In fact, the only new method of cooking is by pressure cooker. All other implements, and gimmicks, work on old principles, including even the blender which does in a trice the work of a mixer, or your own wrist wielding a large fork. Electricity merely replaces your own energy; it does not change the method of work.

If you're into collecting old kitchen utensils, or want to start, you should have some idea of what to look for. Nineteenth century cookware is still plentiful; Edwardian, with its new-fangled electrical appliances, more so.

Early kitchenware was made of copper, later lined with tin as people realized the danger of cooking in unlined copper and the possibility of death by poison from the green, powdery growth, verdigris.

There was of course no bakelite or plastic available in the nineteenth century, so kitchen gadgets, such as choppers and even knife sharpeners, were made of wood and metal. I own a Victorian potato slicer which is beautifully finished, with a patina like velvet. It cost a dime in a junk store, and so did its cousin of an earlier date.

Obviously, these gadgets were often immersed in water, but a good rubdown with pure lemon oil will restore their usually dried-out surfaces. This treatment will also preserve the wooden handles of steel knives —those robustly made, weatherbeaten antiques which you can hone and use like new.

Electrical appliances of early vintage also abound in junky antique stores. The easiest to find is the waffle iron; occasionally, however, a treasure of an old toaster will come to light—its hinged metal doors decorated in a lacy design of cut-out work, an odd reminder that lace was the decorative rage around the turn of the century.

As you collect, you'll be surprised how modern

these oldtime kitchen utensils look, particularly the
Dover egg beater. This handy gadget surely hangs in
your kitchen right now; only its brand name will be
new, for the design of the egg beater has not changed
in near on a hundred years, perhaps more. Other
gadgets you'll find that have stood the test of time are
the melon scoop, the double boiler (known earlier as
the "farina" boiler), the colander and the ice cream
freezer—and we're overlooking sundry frying pans,
pots, and saucepans, and that standby of the nineteenth-century cook, the *bain-marie*.

Can you use antique utensils? Certainly—provided
they're made of safe materials such as cast iron, tin-
lined copper, porcelainized metal, or silver as Mr.
Francatelli directs in a cheese recipe. If they pass the
eagle-eye of your electrician, you can use your electrical ancients too; if unsafe, sometimes they can be
rewired.

Incidentally, appliances and gadgets of the pre-
World War I era often have their patent date stamped
on the bottom, a sure clue to vintage.

The Safest Cookware, Old and New

FROM the health point of view, the safest cookware is
made of stainless steel, pyrex glass, porcelained iron,
terracotta, and copper lined with stainless steel. Tin
is also safe, and so is cast iron. Aluminum is still con-
troversial, and for this reason I hesitate to recommend
it.

Copper lined with steel is expensive; but it lasts so
long you can bequeath it in your will. In fact, divided
by its years of use, the cost of copper cookware is
actually little, particularly if your favorite pan is a
relined antique from the year 18-something. Then,
too, when heated copper's soft, even temperature lulls
rather than cooks—as chefs and housewives have
known through the ages.

2

*Soups, Sauces,
And Tasty Morsels*

A Fasting-Day Soop.

TAKE Spinnage, Sorrel, Chervil and Lettuce, and chop them a little; then brown some Butter, and put in your Herbs, keep them stirring that they do not burn; then have boiling Water over the fire, and put to it a very little Pepper, some Salt, a whole Onion stuck with Cloves, and a *French* Roll cut in slices and dried very hard, and some Pistachia kernels blanched and shred fine, and let all boil together; then beat up the yolks of eight Eggs with a little White-wine and the juice of a Lemon, and mix it with your Broth, and toast a whole *French* Roll, and put in the middle of your dish, and pour your Soop over it; garnish your dish with ten or twelve poached Eggs and scalded Spinnage.

Eliza Smith's *The Compleat Housewife*, 1727

Oldtime Soups—Nourishing Meals in Miniature

～～～～～～～～～～～～～～～～～～～～

"Beau-ootiful Soo-oop!
Soo-oop of the e-e-evening,
Beautiful, beauti-FUL SOUP!"

THUS sang Lewis Carroll in praise of soup—in this case, turtle. But Eliza Smith's green vegetable soup (above) inspires paeans, too, for there are few dishes as delectable as a bowl of filling, old-fashioned pottage.

Back in 1727, however, Eliza Smith prepared her delicate soup only for fast days, even though it was laced with eggs, pistachio nuts, and bread. For feast days she undoubtedly served her Crawfish or Lobster Soop, a truly splendid concoction into which she threw one carp, baked first in the oven, and a hundred crawfish, adding a clutch of forcemeat balls for good measure.

By the end of the nineteenth century, great chefs like Francatelli made bowls of soup their overture to the grand orgy of dinner—artistic hints of gourmet delights in future courses. But that, of course, was yesterday.

Today, we again sit down to a steaming plateful of soup—eye-appealing, nose-appealing, and infinitely "beau-ootiful," a repast in its own right.

The soups presented on the following pages are mostly meatless and easily made with natural foods; some are cooked with a vegetable base, others with milk or cereal, or even fruit—and one, would you believe it, with beer.

So plop a couple of Egg Balls, or other tasty, protein-rich morsels, into Mrs. Gillette's Onion Soup; or

dish up a nourishing meal in miniature, like this Pea
Soup created by Miss T. S. Shute a century ago.

Pea Soup

Miss Shute's *American Housewife*,
1879

"Put a pint of split peas to soak overnight. About
three hours before dinner pour off the water and add
two quarts of water, a carrot, an onion, a little celery
or celery-seed, and a small piece of salt pork. Boil it
steadily, and be careful to stir it often, lest it should
burn; have boiling water at hand to add, as the water
boils away much faster in pea soup than in any other
kind; strain it through a coarse sieve; a cup of milk
added after the soup is done is an improvement. Serve
with toasted bread."

Cook it in that chef's friend, the double boiler;
watch the water in the lower half, adding more *boiling*
water as necessary.

Don't throw out the water used to soak the peas—
it acquires vitamins. Add fresh water to make two
quarts.

Natural foods ingredients to serve ten:

1 pt (2 c) split peas
2 qt (8 c) water
1 large carrot
1 large onion

1 celery stalk *or*
  1 tsp seed
1 small piece salt pork
sea salt (if needed)
1 c fresh milk

You can add:

1 tbsp yeast extract in place of salt pork
dried milk, reconstituted, in place of fresh, with a
  knob of butter or margarine

∾

The White House Cook Book, despite its aristocratic title, features many inexpensive down-to-earth dishes, thanks I'm sure to the wifely expertise of Mrs. Gillette, the homemaking half of the cooking duo of Ziemann and Gillette. One of her homier soup recipes features that classic combination, onions and milk.

Some people regard the onion and its first cousin, garlic, as cure-alls. Actually, both these bulb herbs are strongly diuretic, which may account for their popularity as so-called remedies for ailments ranging from dropsy to flatulence to vertigo. Remedy or not, onions are darned good eating, as the French well know and Mrs. Gillette proves with her own Onion Soup.

Onion Soup

Hugo Ziemann and Mrs. Gillette's
White House Cook Book, 1887

"One quart of milk, six large onions, yolks of four eggs, three tablespoonfuls of butter, a large one of flour, one cupful of cream, salt, pepper. Put the butter in a frying pan. Cut the onions into thin slices and drop in the butter. Stir until they begin to cook; then cover tight and set back, where they will simmer, but not burn, for half an hour. Now put the milk on to boil, and then add the dry flour to the onions and stir constantly for three minutes over the fire; then turn the mixture into the milk and cook fifteen minutes. Rub the soup through a strainer [blend], return to the fire, season with salt and pepper. Beat the yolks of the eggs well, add the cream to them and stir into the soup. Cook three minutes, stirring constantly. If you have no cream, use milk, in which case add a tablespoonful of butter at the same time. Pour over fried croutons in a soup tureen.

"This is a refreshing dish when one is fatigued."

Natural foods ingredients to serve eight to ten:

3 tbsp butter or margarine	pepper
6 large onions	yolks of 4 eggs
1 qt milk	1 c cream (or milk *plus* 1 tbsp butter or margarine)
1 heaping tbsp whole-wheat flour	croutons (see CROUTONS)
sea salt	

To turn into French Onion Soup:

Forget the croutons, serve in individual fire-proof bowls. Grate Parmesan cheese over each and pop under the broiler until the cheese browns—a minute or so.

✌

The Irishman is noted for his good looks, stalwart physique, and poetic genius. Which is not surprising—the staple food of Ireland is traditionally the potato, a king amongst vegetables. High in vitamin C (cooked, they hold enough to halt scurvy), potatoes contain a small amount of protein, much potassium, and A and B vitamins.

To conserve these nutrients, bake your potatoes jacketed, in the oven or in a potato baker. Boil them unpeeled—the skins will break into snippets imperceptible when mashed, blended, or sieved.

Here is Mrs. Gillette's truly Irish Potato Soup:

Irish Potato Soup

Hugo Ziemann and Mrs. Gillette's
White House Cook Book, 1887

". . . boil eight medium-sized potatoes with a large onion, sliced, some herbs, salt and pepper; press all through a colander; then thin it with rich milk and add a lump of butter, more seasoning, if necessary; let it heat well and serve hot."

Flavor with mint, thyme, or one of the more exotic herbs, such as nasturtium or yerba buena (the latter with a frugal touch).

For a hearty serving, allow one potato per person and one sliced onion to four servings or less. Boil in to a soup consistency, adding the other ingredients.

Reheat and serve, adding chopped greenery, such as parsley or watercress, for garnish. Serves eight."

You can add:

leftover watercress or celery tops, chopped as garnish or cooked in as part of the mixture.

❧

Leftover—use or throw out? That's the quandary of every economizing, but vitamin-conscious cook.

The following recipe, from the five-volume series of cookbooks edited by Marion Harland and Christine Terhune Herrick, takes care of a surplus of cooked root or gourd vegetables with the least possible recooking.

Squash Soup

Marion Harland and Christine
Herrick's *Modern Cooking*, 1904

"One cupful of cold boiled squash run through a colander; beat into this 1 teaspoonful each of salt and of sugar, a little pepper and a pinch of mace, 1 tablespoonful of onion juice, and 2 of minced celery. Place this on the stove, stirring constantly until it becomes very hot.

"Have ready a quart of heated milk. . . . Stir 2 tablespoonfuls of butter and 1 of flour into the milk [gradually]. Mix the hot squash and the milk well together in the tureen and serve.

"Turnip soup can be made in the same way."

Natural foods ingredients to serve four:

1 c cold boiled squash
1 tsp sea salt
1 tsp turbinado sugar
a little pepper
pinch of mace
1 tbsp onion juice

2 tbsp minced celery
1 qt milk
2 tbsp butter or margarine
1 tbsp wholewheat flour

You can add:

2 tbsp soybean flour for protein balance.
Any root vegetable instead of squash.

∾

Soups made with herbs culled from a garden aromatic with thyme and basil—and perhaps stiff-necked lavender, whose perfumed oil you pinch out with your fingers—belong in oldtime cookbooks.

Try this herb soup, even if you pluck your herbs, dried and jarred, at the local health store.

Soup of Herbs with Parmesan

Marion Harland and Christine
Herrick's *Modern Cooking*, 1904

"Wash in several waters a handful each of chervil, chives, and sorrel, and a head of tender celery; add a very little tarragon and a few sprigs of parsley. Drain all these free from water and cut them in small pieces. Put them in a saucepan and pour over 3 pints of clear stock or broth, and boil until all are tender."

Before serving sprinkle with grated Parmesan cheese; and pass around the wholegrain toast.

Natural foods ingredients to serve six:

handful each of chervil, chives, sorrel	1 sprig tarragon
	6 sprigs parsley
1 head celery minus outer leaves	3 pt (6 c) clear stock or broth

You can add:

Vegetable in place of clear stock, or 3 pt water and 1½ tbsp yeast extract.

2 tbsp dried vegetables, available at many health stores.

3 tbsp grated Parmesan cheese.

❧

Lafcadio Hearn, more compiler than cookbook writer, is one of those personalities that shine through the decades. Indeed, few writers can boast of Greek, Irish, English, American, and finally, Japanese influences on their work—and not overlooking the colorful Latin atmosphere of New Orleans, where he created his classic *La Cuisine Créole*.

Born in Greece in 1850 of an Anglo-Irish father and a Greek mother, Lafcadio led a checkered life, working as a newspaperman in the United States—a country he virtually adopted, at least for a while. Fascinated by Japanese art and culture (which he wrote about later for his U.S. audience), this true cosmopolitan married a Japanese girl, took her name, and settled down in his next, and last, adopted country, Japan. He wrote his famous cookbook sometime before 1885 while working as a reporter.

La Cuisine Créole makes delightful reading—and cooking—and you'll find it hard to track down a first edition.

Lafcadio's delicious Shrimp Gombo is hardly meager, and good any Lenten or other day. It's one of several real Southern recipes featured in his charming book.

Maigre Shrimp Gombo for Lent

Lafcadio Hearn's *La Cuisine Créole*,
1885

"Boil a pint of shrimps in a quart of water; give them only one boil up, then set them to drain and cool, reserving the water they were boiled in. Chop up three dozen okra pods, two onions, a pod of pepper, and a little parsley, and fry them brown in a little [oil] or butter; add to the okra the shrimps and the strained water in which they were boiled. Let all boil for an hour, and season with salt and pepper to taste. When shrimp and crabs cannot be procured, half a pound of [salt] codfish, soaked an hour or two, and chopped fine, will do very well. All gombo should be thickend with a little flour—browned, if preferred—and stirred in just before adding the water; then boil an hour."

If using salt codfish, soak skin side up in cold water for twenty-four hours, changing the water five or six times. Simmer for half an hour, then de-bone and chop fine. Reserve the water and proceed as with the cooked shrimp above.

Natural foods ingredients to serve six to eight:

1 pt shrimp (about 1 lb) a little oil or butter for
   or ½ lb salt codfish   frying
1 qt water   sea salt
36 okra pods   pepper
2 medium onions   a little wholewheat flour
1 green pepper   for thickening
1 tbsp chopped parsley

You can add:

red bell pepper for a beautiful, brightly colored dish.

℞

If you're vegetarian, you'll enjoy the following bean and nut soups as good sources of protein.

Beans, of course, are legumes and so are peanuts—both of which, despite their richness, are incomplete protein. I suggest, therefore, that you add a sprinkling of sunflower or sesame seeds, which provide the amino acids to make the proteins in legumes complete—an important factor if you're depending on vegetables for protein. (For more on the subject of balancing up proteins, see Frances Moore Lappé's *Diet For A Small Planet*, Ballantine, 1971.)

On the other hand, almonds can supply the protein in a vegetarian diet. In fact, they're so rich that non-vegetarians getting their proteins from animal sources should eat but few—twenty grams of almonds (fifteen to twenty nuts) have approximately the nutritive value of one egg. So be circumspect in your use of these delicious nuts.

But first this bean recipe—which belongs in your Lazy/Leftovers Folder:

Baked Bean Soup

Marion Harland and Christine
Herrick's *Modern Cooking*, 1904

"To a pint of baked beans add 1 quart water and a slice of onion; boil to a pulp, mash [better, blend without cooking] and season. An equal part of [cooked] sweet corn may be added."

Heat in a double boiler and serve piping hot with wholewheat toast. You'll have enough for four, with seconds.

You can add:

a pinch of cayenne (Mrs. Henderson's idea) *or* Francatelli's AROMATIC HERBACEOUS SEASONING.

❧

Black Bean Soup

Miss Parloa's *New Cook Book*, 1880

"A pint of black beans, soaked over night in three quarts of water. In the morning pour off this water [and to it add more water to make 12 cups again]. Boil gently six hours. When done, there should be one quart [of water]. Add a quart of stock, six whole cloves, six whole allspice, a small piece of mace, a small piece of cinnamon, stalk of celery, a bouquet of sweet herbs, also one good-sized onion and one small slice each of turnip and carrot, all cut fine and fried in three tablespoonfuls of butter. Into the butter remaining in the pan put a spoonful of flour, and cook until brown. Add to soup, and simmer all together one hour. Season with salt and pepper, and rub through a fine sieve. Serve with slices of lemon and egg balls, the lemon to be put in the tureen with the soup."

Natural foods ingredients to serve a houseful of people:

1 pt (2 cups) black beans
water (see above)
4 c stock or water with yeast or vegetable extract
6 whole cloves
6 whole *or* 1¼ tsp ground allspice
1 small piece of mace *or* 1 tsp powdered mace
1 small piece of stick cinnamon

1 stalk celery
1 bouquet garnis
1 good-sized onion
1 small slice turnip
1 small carrot
3 tbsp butter
1 tbsp wholewheat flour
sea salt
pepper
1 lemon
12 egg balls (see EGG BALLS)

You can add:

6 dozen hard-boiled eggs halved in place of Egg Balls or 12 hard-boiled eggs, the whites removed, dropped in whole.

❧

Nut and Tomato Soup

Marion Harland and Christine
Herrick's *Modern Cooking*, 1904

"1 pint of strained cooked tomatoes; 1 pint water;
1 pint milk; 2 tablespoonfuls of peanut butter.

"Put the nut butter in a dish and add a little
water; rub smooth with a spoon, and add a little
more water until it is of the consistency of thick
cream. Put the tomatoes, water, and prepared [pea-
nut] butter on the fire and let boil ten minutes. When
ready to take off add the milk, and season with salt
and cayenne.

"Instead of the nut butter, . . . [1 cup] roasted
and shelled peanuts may be used, or one-half peanuts
and one-half chestnuts or pecans. Remove the brown
husks from the peanuts, pound to a paste in a mortar
with a little hot water, add a little cream or milk,
blending thoroughly; then proceed the same as with
the nut butter."

When straining the tomatoes, reserve the liquid and
add to the water, making one pint (2 cups).

Caution: Use only *unsalted* peanuts and/or nuts.

Natural foods ingredients to serve four to six:

1 pt (2 c) cooked or
canned tomatoes,
strained
1 pt (2 c) water *plus* a
little
1 pt (2 c) milk

2 tbsp peanut butter *or*
1 c roasted and shelled
peanuts *or* ½ c peanuts
and ½ c chestnuts or
pecans, mixed
sea salt to taste
pinch cayenne

You can add:

dried milk reconstituted in place of fresh.

～

Almond Milk Soup

Marion Harland and Christine
Herrick's *Modern Cooking*, 1904

"Blanch ½ pound of almonds and brown in the oven; while crisp and hot, mash to a powder with a rolling pin. Scald 1 quart of milk, add a tablespoonful of butter rolled in a tablespoonful of flour, and the almonds. Cook five minutes, add a teaspoonful of salt and a dash of cayenne, and serve hot with croutons."

Take the easy way—"mash" the nuts, browned of course, in your nut grinder. Serve with an alkali food (almonds are acid) like carrots or green vegetables.

Natural foods ingredients to serve six:

½ lb almonds
1 qt (4 cups) milk
1 tbsp butter or
    margarine

1 tbsp wholewheat flour
1 tsp. sea salt
dash cayenne
croutons (see CROUTONS)

You can add:

cashew nuts in place of almonds;
dried milk reconstituted in place of fresh.

A touch of Golden Africa in a nineteenth-century dining-room? Yes, indeed, in the Peanut Soup (below), which combines two flavors dear to African taste: peanuts and fish, in this case peanut butter and oysters. Incidentally, this combination was budget in those far-off days, when oysters and peanuts vied for bottom rung on the money ladder.

Nevertheless, the combination is excellent and an interesting change, even though oysters have catapulted into the luxury class.

Peanut Soup

Marion Harland and Christine
Herrick's *Modern Cooking*, 1904

"Since the many really good preparations of nuts, in the form of nut butter, have been put on the market, nut soups may be quickly made. These soups are said to have a distinctly meaty flavor, that of nuts being partially transformed in the blending with the other ingredients. For an emergency soup the following is one of the most easily made:

"One-half cup of peanut butter; 1 pint milk; liquor strained from 1 pint of oysters. Salt and paprika.

"Rub the peanut butter to a smooth paste with a little of the milk, and add, stirring thoroughly, the remainder of the milk [heated]; put over the fire and simmer slowly until it thickens, then add the hot oyster liquor, which has been brought to a boil and skimmed. Add the seasoning and serve with [wholegrain] crackers.

"Instead of the oyster liquor the juice may be strained from a can of tomatoes. Bring it to a boil. . . ."

And those expensive, leftover oysters: use in Virginia Oyster Soup, or as additions to any oyster recipe. Or make a plain sauce, add the oysters, and pour over boiled natural brown rice. If it's his birthday, treat the cat.

❧

Our forbears invariably served oysters to wilting maidens (probably tubercular, sad to say) and other invalids "to build up strength"—and Isadora Duncan's mother (according to Isadora) consumed quarts of the delicious little shellfish when carrying her gifted baby. Certainly, oysters contain valuable protein, are easily digested, but also very acid.

So eat this soup joyously but sparingly, in honor of the great and fabulous dancer—even though it's named "Virginia," not "Isadora."

Virginia Oyster Soup

Marion Harland and Christine
Herrick's *Modern Cooking*, 1904

"Take 1 quart of good oysters and wash through two waters. Strain the liquor and add to it 2 blades of mace, a stalk of celery chopped fine, ½ teaspoonful of white pepper, a few grains of cayenne, and salt if necessary. Simmer over the fire five minutes, then add 2 tablespoonfuls of butter rubbed smooth with 2 tablespoonfuls of flour and a pint and a half of rich cream and new milk, half and half. Let it come to a good boil, stirring all the time; then put in the oysters, and let them boil up once and no more, or they will shrivel and toughen. Pour into a hot tureen and give thanks."

Natural foods ingredients to serve four to six:

1 qt oysters (about 4 c)
2 blades (a large pinch) mace
stalk of celery, chopped fine
½ tsp white pepper
a few grains of cayenne pepper

sea salt to taste
2 tbsp butter
2 tbsp wholewheat flour
1½ c heavy cream
1½ c fresh milk

❧

Insight into the personal, often closed, lives of royalty and other personages of exalted rank is always fascinating, and often surprising in revelations of character and remote ways of life.

For all the pomp that surrounded her overstuffed court (in both the figurative and gourmet sense), Queen Victoria obviously yearned for the simple life —or so her choice of soup, prepared by the ever-loyal Francatelli, seems to imply.

Have cereal soups extra-strengthening qualities? Perhaps. At least, two famous women, Queen Victoria and Jenny Lind, each tremendously powerful in her own sphere, swore by their own special recipes, reproduced here for your own experimenting.

Victoria Soup

Francatelli's *Cook's Guide*, 1888

"Wash and scald half a pound of Frankfort pearl barley, and put this into a stewpan with three pints of good white veal stock, and simmer it very gently over a slow fire for an hour and a half; by which time the barley will be nearly dissolved; remove a third of it into a small soup-pot; rub the remainder through a tammy or sieve [or blend], pour it to the whole barley; add half a pint of cream; season with a little salt; stir it over the fire until hot, and serve.

"This soup may be prepared also with rice; they are, or at least *were*, the only soups eaten by the Queen when I had the honour of waiting on Her Majesty."

As barley is excessively acid, make this royal soup with neutralizing vegetable stock.

Natural foods ingredients to serve six:

½ lb pearl barley *or* rice   ½ pt (1 c) cream
3 pt (6 c) stock   sea salt to taste

You can add:

milk instead of cream; if dried reconstituted, add a
  knob of butter or margarine;
1 cup raisins—delicious and alkalizing; and a little
  chopped parsley for a spot of color.

Jenny Lind, the Swedish Nightingale whose name
is magic even today, came to America for a two-year
tour in 1850 backed by that Sol Hurok of the nineteenth century, P. T. Barnum. La Lind was a superb
musician and actress (she'd acted professionally before she sang); her forte, however, was the oratorio,
and to the extraordinary tonal qualities of her voice
was added a moving depth of feeling, for she was
truly religious.

Undoubtedly the greatest singer in the world of the
past, Mme. Lind was a charming but bluntly forthright woman whose comments often surprised the
good-mannered Americans of her day.

Here is the favorite soup of that extraordinary
singer, whose voice is lost in the chords of the nineteenth century; may its strengthening qualities bring
good luck to all would-be Jenny Linds.

Jenny Lind's Soup

Marion Harland and Christine
Herrick's *Modern Cooking*, 1904

"Wash ¼ pound best pearl sago till the water
poured off is clear, then cook, till tender and thick, in
a quart of cold water or broth, which should be
heated slowly. Mix gradually with this a pint of
boiling cream and the yolks of 4 fresh eggs, then add
2 quarts of strong veal or beef stock, boiling hot.
Serve at once."

Clearly, Mme. Lind was a company-loving soul—there's enough soup here to fill up twelve *fin de siècle* Brünnhildes.

Natural foods ingredients to serve twelve generously:

¼ lb pearl sago
1 qt (4 c) water or stock
1 pt (2 c) light cream
4 egg yolks

2 qt (8 c) beef or veal stock
sea salt
pepper

You can add:

yeast or vegetable extract and equivalent amount of water in place of meat stock.

Here's a spiced-up version of a simple cereal soup.

Velvet Soup

Marion Harland and Christine
Herrick's *Modern Cooking*, 1904

"Cook 1 tablespoonful of pearl tapioca or sago, previously soaked in cold water, in a quart of [salted] clear stock or bouillon. When the tapioca is cooked clear, beat the yolk of 3 eggs lightly, put them in the tureen, and pour the soup over, stirring until it becomes uniformly smooth and creamy; add a dash of nutmeg and paprika. . . ."

Natural foods ingredients to serve four generously:

1 tbsp pearl tapioca or sago
a little cold water
1 qt (4 c) stock or bouillon

sea salt to taste
3 fertilized egg yolks
pinch of grated nutmeg
pinch of paprika

You can add:

1 quart water and vegetable extract in place of stock or bouillon. *Don't* use yeast extract.

Fruit soups make a refreshing change, and are easily fixed with arrowroot or cereal for thickening. Marion Harland, best-selling novelist turned cookbook author, waxes poetic on the subject:

Fruit Soups

Marion Harland and Christine
Herrick's *Modern Cooking*, 1904

"On a blistering hot day fruit soups served very cold are sometimes more acceptable than one that must be served very hot to be palatable. For this purpose cherries, apricots, peaches, plums and other meaty fruits are best. They may be used separately for a soup that takes its name from the fruit used, or may be combined and called simply fruit soup or given a more fanciful name from some flavoring used.

"These soups are only slightly sweetened, as the tartness is an agreeable preface to a hot-day dinner.

"1 pint crushed fruit; 1 pint water; ¼ pint red wine or ½ [wine] glassful currant or raspberry jelly; a stick of cinnamon; a blade of mace; juice and a little grated rind of lemon; 2 tablespoonfuls sugar; 2 tablespoonfuls arrowroot.

"Stew the fruit in the water until soft, crack a few of the stones, and add the kernels while cooking. Strain through a coarse strainer, using a silver spoon to press the pulp through the strainer. Put back into the saucepan; add the lemon juice, sugar, and arrowroot, which has been mixed with cold water, stirring constantly until it thickens. Let it cook until the arrowroot is clear. Add the jelly; and stir until dissolved. Take from the fire and cool, then add the wine, and put on the ice until thoroughly chilled. Serve in bouillon cups, with bits of cracked ice and a few whole cherries or firm red raspberries to each cup.

"Small triangles of buttered toast, or toasted wafers, may be served as an adjunct.

"Should the water boil down while the fruit is cooking, add more. It should be the consistency of a thick fruit syrup when strained."

Three cups of fruit, de-stoned and cut into pieces, cooked in two cups of water will make a nice mush.

Natural foods ingredients to serve six:

1 pt (2 c) fruit *without* stones
a few fruit-stone kernels
1 pt (2 c) water
¼ pt (½ c) red wine *or* ½ wineglass (2 tbsp) currant or raspberry jelly
1 stick cinnamon
1 blade, or pinch, of mace

1 lemon, juice and rind
2 tbsp turbinado sugar
2 tbsp. arrowroot
whole cherries or red raspberries for decoration
small triangles of wholewheat toast

❧

You can top your menu with this Sago and/or Fruit Soup from Hawaii, or serve a thicker version as dessert.

Sago Soup
(Hawaiian Recipe)

Marion Harland and Christine
Herrick's *Modern Cooking*, 1904

"Wash ¼ cup pearl sago through several cold waters; cook slowly in 1 quart water till the sago is transparent; add a pinch of salt, a 2-inch piece stick cinnamon, ½ cup seeded and chopped raisins; and just before serving ½ pint of fruit juice and 2 tablespoonfuls sugar."

Natural foods ingredients to serve four:

¼ c pearl sago
  1 qt (4 c) water
pinch sea salt
2-inch piece stick
    cinnamon

½ c raisins, seeded and
  chopped
½ pt (1 c) fruit juice
2 tbsp turbinado sugar

You can add:

a dollop of ice cream or yogurt if served cold as dessert;

also, try apple or apricot juice—both blend well in this recipe.

❧

Need a conversation-piece soup, or an inexpensive Tom and Jerry? Here's the very concoction:

Beer Soup
(German Method)

Marion Harland and Christine
Herrick's *Modern Cooking*, 1904

"Simmer 2 quarts of mild beer (it should not be bitter) with the thin rind of a lemon, a few cloves, and a stick of cinnamon; sweeten with sugar, and add it, through a sieve, to the well-beaten yolks of 6 eggs and half a pint of (heavy) cream. Whilst pouring into the tureen, stir into a froth with a wire whisk.

"The beer should be very hot, but not boiling, when stirred into the eggs. Serve hot with toast. Time, about half an hour to simmer. There will be sufficient of this for eight or ten persons."

You can add:

apple juice in place of beer; but beer's wackier.

And this soup, which is simpler to fix than it looks, will do you proud in the grand manner. Serve it in your most impressive tureen.

Consommé à l'Impératrice
(An Elaborate Dinner Soup)

Marion Harland and Christine
Herrick's *Modern Cooking*, 1904

"Put a level tablespoonful each of butter and flour into a saucepan with ½ cup milk, stir till it boils, and add ½ teaspoonful onion juice, 1 tablespoonful chopped parsley, ½ saltspoonful mace, salt and pepper, and ½ cup chopped [cooked] chicken; mix thoroughly and turn out to cool. At serving time make this into small balls, roll in egg, and drop quickly into hot fat or oil and drain on soft brown paper. Have ½ pint of fresh green peas and 4 table-spoonfuls [measured raw] rice carefully boiled, and put in soup tureen—turn in hot chicken consomme—drop in the forcemeat balls, and serve at once."

Natural foods ingredients to serve six:

Forcemeat balls

1 tbsp butter	sea salt
1 tbsp wholewheat flour	pepper
½ cup fresh milk	½ cup cooked chicken,
½ tsp onion juice	chopped
1 tbs chopped parsley	1 egg, well beaten
pinch powdered mace	oil for frying

Soup base

1 cup green peas, cooked	3 cups chicken consommé
1 cup cooked natural brown rice (from 4 tbsp raw rice)	sea salt to taste

Some Great and Useful Sauces

To great chefs of the nineteenth century—Francatelli, Escoffier, and Filippini of Delmonico's—it was perfection of the sauce that counted, for it was in its creation that these cooks sailed into a culinary heaven. Escoffier, in *Guide Culinaire*, devotes about fifty pages to this subject.

Today, we're more objective. We don't see sauce as a hallowed necessity, but as something to brighten a dish, or round it off nutritionally. Nevertheless, you'll find a small quantity of a few basic sauces mighty useful. (If you own a freezer, freeze in ice-cube trays: one cube equals a serving.)

Maestro Francatelli, who clearly regards his readers as naughty children apt to bollix the job, has some hints you may find helpful:

On Sauce-Making

Francatelli's *Cook's Guide*, 1888

"*Note:* Allow me here to impress upon your minds how all-important it is that whenever you are stirring a sauce upon the fire, you must bear with some strength and a little tact on the edge of the bowl of the wooden spoon, so as to prevent the sauce from burning at the bottom of the stewpan while it is being reduced; for rest assured that whenever through negligence this occurs, the sauce is spoilt. These remarks apply more especially to such sauces as contain milk or cream."

And keep the flame low, adding the milk cautiously, a little at a time.

❧

Tomato, fish, butter, arrowroot, and white sauces make excellent bases to which you can add your own special herbs and flavorings. Francatelli's Tomato Sauce, for example, well curried up (see CURRY POWDER) is excellent poured over a bowlful of rice.

Francatelli's Tomato Sauce (Adapted)

Blend together one medium can of tomatoes, a small can of tomato paste, finely sliced shallots, a bay leaf and a pinch of thyme, a teaspoonful of anchovy (or 1 inch of anchovy paste in a tube), a little oil, a teaspoonful of sugar or honey, and the juice of half a lemon. No cooking needed, of course, unless you use fresh tomatoes, which will need to be boiled in a little water for five minutes. (Leave the skins on, and if necessary, cut into little pieces with scissors.)

Francatelli's curry sauce, as expected, has an extra something—a bit of glaze.

Indian Sauce

Francatelli's *Cook's Guide*, 1888

"For half a pint of Tomato Sauce, add a tablespoonful of diluted and strained curry-paste, a bit of glaze, and a little anchovy; boil together and serve."

A most useful sauce. Use Mr. Francatelli's own Tomato Sauce or tomato paste as base; add a teaspoonful of honey for glaze, a pinch or more of curry powder, and a few drops of vegetable oil.

As a natural foods cook, get together with Chef Francatelli to make white sauce—usually a flaccid bore—into a tasty, nutritious, and interesting beautifier.

Make up a pint periodically, with wholegrain flour, of course, to use as a base for herb sauces such as parsley or watercress; or for enrichment with protein such as soybean curd or crumbled hard-boiled egg.

Economical White Sauce

Francatelli's Cook's Guide, 1888

"Mix well in a stewpan two ounces of flour, one ounce of butter, a little nutmeg, pepper and salt; to these add a pint of milk, stir over the fire for ten minutes, and strain off for use."

The secret's in the last phrase—straining will of course remove any suspicion of lumps, and incidentally make a smoother sauce.

Natural foods ingredients to make three cups sauce:

2 oz (¼ c) wholewheat flour	pepper
1 oz butter	sea salt
a little nutmeg, grated	1 pt (2 c) milk

You can add:

cream instead of milk, plus one beaten egg yolk; this turns White Sauce into Cream Sauce;
1 or 2 extra tbs of flour for a medium or thick sauce;
for enrichment: a little wheat germ or sunflower meal —which, incidentally, will thicken the sauce. So start with the thin version, above.

Note: White Sauce made with wholewheat flour has a chewy texture and a beigey color. For a smoother, whiter-looking sauce, use wholewheat flour, pastry grind.

❧

And here's the great Francatelli's version of another sauce that's passed into the culinary repertoire:

Melted Butter, or Butter Sauce

Francatelli's *Cook's Guide*, 1888

"Knead two ounces of fresh butter with one ounce of flour in a small stewpan; add a gill of water; season with a little pepper and salt, and stir over the fire until the sauce thickens, but do not allow it to boil; finish by working into it a bit more butter, and serve."

Natural foods ingredients to make one cup sauce:

2 oz sweet butter, plus a little   grind
1 oz (2 tbsp) whole-wheat flour, pastry   1 gill (¼ c) water
  a little pepper
  pinch of sea salt

You can add:

shellfish (see below);
chopped onion;
parsley for parsley butter, etc.

❧

It was with shellfish sauces like these that Francatelli and his confrères turned bowls of simple rice into dishes fit for emperors (there were several actively ruling in those golden days of monarchy). The sauces are delicious, too, over spaghetti or vegetables such as broccoli.

Lobster Sauce

Francatelli's *Cook's Guide*, 1888

"Split a lobster, remove the pith, coral and spawn to be pounded with an equal proportion of butter in a mortar, and afterwards rubbed through a hair sieve on a plate; break the shell, and having removed all the meat, cut it into large or small square pieces, according to fancy. Next, prepare some melted butter [see above]; to this add the spawn and the lobster, season with the juice of half a lemon, a teaspoonful of anchovy, and a pinch of cayenne pepper, and serve hot."

❧

Shrimp Sauce

Francatelli's *Cook's Guide*, 1888

"Prepare butter sauce [see above]; to this add a teaspoonful of anchovy, a small pinch of cayenne, a little lemon juice, and a bit of lobster butter to colour and flavor it; lastly, throw in the picked shrimps, and serve hot."

Heat until the shrimp are cooked—about five minutes.

Don't get *distrait* if you're out of lobster butter; either add more shrimp or add color by sprinkling paprika over the sauce before serving. Or both.

Natural foods ingredients to make three cups sauce:

1 c BUTTER SAUCE	pinch cayenne
1 tsp anchovy (or 1 inch anchovy paste)	a little lemon juice
	1 cup prepared shrimp

~❧~

Arrowroot Sauce

Francatelli's *Cook's Guide*, 1888

"To a tablespoonful of arrowroot add twice that quantity of sugar, a [wine] glass of wine, the juice of half a lemon, and nearly half a pint of milk or water; stir this quickly over the fire until it boils.

"*Note:* This sauce may also be prepared in an almost infinite variety of ways, by using, instead of wine, milk or water as a liquid to mix with the arrowroot, the juices extracted from almost all kinds of fruits as well as all kinds of liqueurs; and they may also be flavored with vanilla, lemon, orange, etc."

You'll probably find the sauce too sweet, so add sugar to taste.

Natural foods ingredients to make about two cups sauce:

1 tbsp arrowroot	juice of ½ lemon
turbinado sugar to taste	1 c milk or water
1 wineglass (¼ c) wine	

You can add:

almost anything; see Francatelli's comments above.

~❧~

Cold fish is usually served dabbed with mayonnaise; rarely does it get its own sauce. You can repair this gastronomic omission with Lafcadio Hearn's Sauce Froide.

Sauce Froide

Lafcadio Hearn's *La Cuisine Créole*, 1885

"Mince quite fine, some parsley, chervil, tarragon, chives and burnet; mix them in five or six tablespoonfuls of oil, or three yolks of hard-boiled eggs rubbed down smooth; add two tablespoonfuls of vinegar, some made mustard, salt and pepper; beat altogether until it is smooth and thick, and serve in a sauce-boat. A good sauce for fish."

Adjust the quantities of herbs to suit your taste, going easy however, on tarragon. To serve with hot fish, heat gently in a double boiler.

Natural foods ingredients to make about one and one-half cups sauce:

1 tbsp finely minced parsley

1 tbsp finely minced chervil

½ tbsp finely minced tarragon

1 tbsp finely minced chives

1 tbsp finely minced burnet

5 or 6 tbsp soy, peanut, or walnut oil *or* 3 yolks of hard-boiled eggs

2 tbsp apple cider vinegar

a little dry mustard made up

sea salt

a little pepper

You can add:

lemon juice in place of vinegar.

Gooseberries are not a familiar sight in American vegetable or health stores—unfortunately, the gooseberry shrubs are hosts to a fungus-parasite of the lovely white pine, so are unpopular with growers. However, you can get this tart and tasty little fruit (which comes green and red and is grown quite prolifically in England) canned and imported, in specialty stores.

When a sauce made from gooseberries is poured over mackerel, the combination of tartness and richness is truly gourmet stuff.

As a substitute for gooseberries, try greening apples. But believe me, the gooseberries are worth the hunt and cost—and mackerel, anyway, is inexpensive.

Green Gooseberry Sauce

Francatelli's *Cook's Guide*, 1888

"Boil half a pint of green gooseberries, drain off the water; rub them through a hair sieve; put this pulp into a stewpan with a wineglass of green raw sorrel or spinach juice; add a small piece of butter, a pinch of sugar, nutmeg, pepper, and salt; make hot, and serve with boiled or grilled mackerel."

Drain off excess syrup if the gooseberries are canned; add all the ingredients and blend, then heat in a double boiler. Absolutely great.

Note:

The raw sorrel or spinach juice tints the sauce a pretty green. Without this coloring job, your sauce will look dejected.

Natural foods ingredients for two cups sauce:

½ pt (1 c) drained canned or fresh gooseberries

1 wineglass (¼ c) sorrel or spinach juice

1 small piece (2 tsp) butter *or* 2 tsp light oil

turbinado sugar to taste
a pinch of nutmeg
a little pepper
a pinch of sea salt

❧

Tasty Morsels to Drop into Soups and Sauces

No thoughtful cook of Eliza Smith's day would dream of serving soup without enriching the nourishing mess with forcemeat balls.

These fascinating morsels can be made of egg, nuts, poultry, and of course meat, all chopped finely, added to a base, and molded into little balls. You can also make an ersatz meat ball from flour and a protein meal such as soybean, or with a packaged nut-cereal mixture. (See FORCEMEAT BALLS.)

Other oddments, such as croutons or dumplings, when dumped (was that how these potato/wheatflour balls came to be named?) into soup add interest or energy-giving calories—the latter particularly important when filling up children with soup at a midday meal.

Marion Harland and Christine Terhune Herrick probably had youngsters in mind when they created these exciting little extras. It's Maria Parloa, however, who gives the last word on:

Dumplings

Miss Parloa's *New Cook Book*, 1880

"One pint of flour, measured before sifting; [2 teaspoonful baking powder], one of sugar, half a teaspoonful of salt. Mix all thoroughly and run through the sieve. Wet with a small cupful of milk. Sprinkle a little flour on the board. Turn the dough (which should have been stirred into a smooth ball with a spoon) on it, roll to the thickness of half an inch, cut into small cakes, and cook ten minutes.

"By remembering that the soup should be boiling rapidly when the dumplings are put in; that they

should not sink too deep in it; that they should boil
just ten minutes; that the cover should fit tightly, so
that the steam shall not escape; and that the pot
boils all the time, so that the steam is kept up; and by
following the other directions, success in insured."

The dumplings, of course, are raw until cooked with
the soup.

Natural foods ingredients for twenty-four dumplings:

1 pt (2 c) wholewheat flour, pastry grind	1 tsp turbinado sugar
2 tsp baking powder	½ tsp sea salt
	¾ c milk

You can add:

a little wheat germ or a little soybean flour;
a little chopped onion or parsley, or crushed garlic.

❧

Egg Balls

Marion Harland and Christine
Herrick's *Modern Cooking*, 1904

"Two hard-boiled eggs; 1 raw egg; 1 tablespoonful flour or fine cracker crumbs; 2 tablespoonfuls melted butter; ½ teaspoonful salt; a dash of cayenne; a little grated nutmeg; a few drops of lemon juice.

"Rub the boiled egg yolks very smooth, mince one of the whites very fine. Mix together, add the seasoning and flour or crumbs. Stir all together with enough of the slightly beaten raw egg to bind and form into balls the size of a nutmeg (about ¾" in diameter), rolling into the egg and crumbs after shaping. Drop the balls into the boiling soup and cook until firm; about five minutes. Or they may be fried to a golden brown in deep boiling fat. Serve in the tureen with the soup."

Use wholewheat flour, of course, and to conserve vitamin C, sprinkle the lemon juice over just before serving.

Croutons

Marion Harland and Christine
Herrick's *Modern Cooking*, 1904

"Cut bread (stale) into ½ inch slices, remove the crust, and cut into ½ inch strips and then into ½-inch cubes. Fry in hot clarified fat [or oil] until lightly browned, then drain; or place in baking pan in very hot oven, and serve."

No-fat version:

Bake tiny blobs of pulled bread (see PULLED BREAD) and drop into soup, or serve separately.

To round off the perfect vegetarian soup, drop in a few Almond Balls for protein—and excitement.

Like Egg Balls, these "marbles" of concentrated nutrition are excellent in salads and in curry sauces. Make double quantity and store the excess in the refrigerator. They're handy to have ready-cooked.

Consommé Almond

Marion Harland and Christine
Herrick's *Modern Cooking*, 1904

"Blanch and chop fine two dozen almonds; mix with an equal quantity stale bread crumbs; season with ½ saltspoonful salt, and add enough of the white of 2 eggs to bind the whole together; mix thoroughly, and form into tiny balls, roll them in the remaining white of egg, and drop into hot oil—not butter.

". . . Shake till the balls are golden brown, lift with a skimmer, drain for an instant on soft brown paper, then put into tureen and turn over nicely seasoned hot stock."

Natural foods ingredients to make eighteen marble-sized balls:

1 doz. (⅛ cup) almonds, chopped fine
⅛ cup bread crumbs
pinch sea salt
white or 2 fertilized eggs
oil for frying, preferably almond or soybean

❧

For genuine, old-fashioned FORCEMEAT BALLS (made with chicken) see CONSOMMÉ À L'IMPÉRATRICE.

You can use this same recipe to make Fish Balls. Add flakes of any white fish, such as cod or haddock, and substitute a little fennel in place of mace.

3

Hearty Dishes with Chicken, Turkey, and Fish

To stew a Turkey.

TAKE a fine young Turkey, kill'd, pull'd, and drawn; fill the ſkin on the Breaſt with Forc'd-meat, and lard it on the ſides with Bacon: Put into the Belly half an Eſchalot, and two Anchovies, and a little Thyme ſhred ſmall; brown it in a Pan, with a little Butter; when 'tis very brown, put it in a Stew-pan, with ſtrong Gravy, ſome White-wine, or Claret, two or three Anchovies, ſome Mace, Sweet-herbs, a little Pepper, and let it ſtew till 'tis thoroughly enough; then thicken the Liquor with Butter and Eggs; fry ſome *French* Loaves dipp'd in Cream, after the Top and the Crum is taken out; then fill them with ſtew'd Oyſters, or Shrimps, or Cockles, and with them garniſh the Diſh, or with ſliced Lemon. A Hen, Gooſe, or Duck, does well this way.

Eliza Smith's *The Compleat Housewife*, 1727

Chicken and Turkey in the Oldtime Manner

~~~~~~

DOESN'T Mistress Smith's gargantuan Turkey Stew make your mouth water? Packed with goodies—and good ideas. You can try it out in miniature using turkey thighs for smallest quantities.

By the end of the nineteenth century, the American housewife-chefs who contributed to a little book entitled *365 Breakfast Dishes* were fixing pint-size versions of Eliza's poultry and fish recipes for *fin de siècle* breakfasts. Today, times and food styles have changed; we eat less, so these breakfast delicacies make ideal main courses for dinner.

Happy victims of an overblown age, those elegant, corseted contributors worked at housewifery as at an art. Even savory dishes were over-decorated, baroque style—chops sported frills of paper, and trimmings of mashed potato squiggled across chicken and turkey aspics and creamed vegetables, and alongside roasts.

These truly accomplished cooks took pride in careful marketing (the basis of good cooking), digging out triumphantly the freshest of foodstuffs from the heaped-up piles, sniffing and pinching cantaloupe for ripeness, shaking and listening to coconuts for the delicate rattle of milk; and heads cocked, tasting deep-purple grapes.

I wonder how these women would react to the peer-in food wrappers which make us such trusting souls. I can see the outraged Mrs. Gillette tearing apart that plastic for the *real* look-see we're often too meek to demand.

Let's see how Mrs. Gillette and the portly Hugo Ziemann checked the chicken and turkey at their local poulterers.

How to Choose Poultry

Hugo Ziemann and Mrs. Gillette's
White House Cook Book, 1887

"In choosing poultry, select those that are fresh and fat, and the surest way to determine whether they are young, is to try the skin under the leg or wing. If it is easily broken, it is young; or, turn the wing backwards, if the joint yields readily, it is tender. When poultry is young the skin is thin and tender, the legs smooth, the feet moist and limber, the eyes full and bright. The body should be thick and the breast fat. Old turkeys have long hairs, and the flesh is purplish where it shows under the skin on the legs and back. About March they deteriorate in quality."

Moral: Come Spring, buy frozen rather than fresh turkey.

Here's an exotic Indian curry for those who like it hot, made more genuine (and expensive) than usual by the addition of pickles imported from India. Use any kind, but I personally root for Major Grey's.

Indian Burdwan

Marion Harland and Christine
Herrick's *Modern Cooking*, 1904

"A very savory and highly approved Indian dish. The joints of a parboiled fowl are generally used for this dish, but if necessary the remains of chicken or fowls that have been served before, and even rabbit, veal, or lamb may be warmed up in the sauce, for which the following is the recipe:

"Peel and chop very finely 4 shallots and 1 onion. Put them into a stewpan with a small cup of good stock, 1 tablespoonful of the essence of anchovies, a little cayenne, and 1 ounce of butter rolled in flour. Stir over the fire until the sauce is ready to boil, then . . . simmer till the onions are done, adding a small cupful of mixed Indian pickles, cut into less than ½ inch pieces, 1 tablespoonful of chili vinegar, and 1 or 2 [wine] glasses of wine, madeira or sherry. Simmer the sauce to make the pickles tender, and pour in the wine when the fowl is ready to be stewed. Skin and lay the fowl in neat pieces into the stewpan with the sauce, and if the fowl has been only parboiled, stew it gently for fifteen or twenty minutes, but for a thoroughly cooked fowl serve as soon as it is ready to boil, with the juice of a fresh lime. Rice is sometimes served with Burdwan as with curry."

First, get the rice boiling, to finish cooking the same moment as the Burdwan.

For chili vinegar, use a pinch of chili and apple cider vinegar or (preferably) lime juice.

Heap the Burdwan over the rice, and serve.

Note: Good for using up leftover poultry.

Natural foods ingredients to serve six to eight:

2 frying chickens, parboiled	1 oz butter or margarine
4 shallots	a little wholewheat flour
1 onion	½ bottle Indian chutney
¾ c stock	1 tbsp chili vinegar
1 tbsp essence of anchovies (2 inches from tube)	1 or 2 wineglasses (¼ to ½ c) wine, madeira, *or* sherry
pinch cayenne	juice of 1 lime
	8 to 10 c cooked rice

Chopped chicken is a genuine mystery—it's anyone's guess what part of the bird got involved.

Consequently, the next recipe is a tight-budget dream—you can use backs, necks, and wings, for when removed from the bone and chopped fine there's no difference in flavor between the meat cut from these lowly parts and the breast and legs.

Figure on getting 1 pound of boneless meat from 3 pounds assorted "bits." The protein value, of course, remains the same, ranging from 16 to 21 percent.

Pressed Chicken

Hugo Ziemann and Mrs. Gillette's
White House Cook Book, 1887

"Clean and cut up your chickens. Stew in just enough water to cover them. When nearly cooked, season them well with salt and pepper. Let them stew down until the water is nearly all boiled out, and the meat drops easily from the bones. Remove the bones and gristle; chop the meat rather coarsely, then turn it back into the stew-kettle, where the broth was left (after skimming off all fat), and let it heat through again. Turn it into a square bread-pan, placing a platter on the top, and a heavy weight on the platter. This, if properly prepared, will turn out like a mold of jelly and may be sliced in smooth, even slices. The success of this depends upon not having too much water; it will not jelly if too weak, or if the water is allowed to boil away entirely while cooking. A good way to cook old fowls."

Your platter should, of course, fit *inside* the bread-pan.

Leave the cooked chicken in the icebox; the broth will jell and you can then easily remove the fat which coagulates on top.

To remove the meat from the bones easily, take a tip from the chef's assistant—use your fingers.

You'll need your sharpest knife for slicing; if you botch the job, and the jelly flops about, serve it garnish-style around the chicken alternated with sprigs of parsley or watercress.

A passing word about kitchen knives. Gourmet cooks plump for unchromed steel knives, the kind used by chefs throughout the centuries. The modern, unchromed versions, which you may find in first-rate cookware stores (such as Bazar Français in New York City) are expensive, but well worth the extra money. Remember it is the *blunt* knife that tends to slip more than the sharp.

All knives are dangerous implements, so be sure you obey these two important rules: always work the action of the knife *away* from your body and hands; store all knives at a height beyond the reach of children.

Panned Chicken

365 Breakfast Dishes, 1901

"Prepare the chicken as for broiling, slightly flatten it and cover with bits of butter and place it in a moderate oven. When it is nearly done sprinkle with salt and pepper and dredge with flour; return to the oven and brown first on one side then on the other. Keep hot while you make the sauce. Pour a cupful of hot milk into the pan and add 1 tablespoonful of grated bread crumbs, add a few drops of onion [juice]. Stir the sauce vigorously, let it boil 1 minute, turn it over the chicken, garnish with parsley and serve."

A pinch of powdered fennel will bring a subtle touch to the gentle flavor. Add to the flour when dredging.

Natural foods ingredients to serve four:

For the chicken:

1 frying chicken, cut up	pepper
bits (about 1 tbsp) of butter or margarine	1 tbsp wholewheat flour parsley for garnish
sea salt	

For the sauce:

1 c hot milk	a few drops onion juice
1 tbsp grated bread-crumbs	pepper sea salt

You can add:

dried milk reconstituted in place of fresh;
a little oil in place of butter—sesame is good;
a *bouquet garnis* (thyme, parsley, and basil) to the sauce.

❧

Yogurt—or yaghourt, yaghurt, or zoolak—is milk fermented by a beneficent bacillus which "cleans up" putrefaction in the intestinal tract. It's a good idea, therefore, to add yogurt in some form to meat dishes of any kind, including, of course, poultry.

The flavor of the following dish (which should be rechristened Dinner Chicken) is delicately sharpened by the addition of yogurt; or add sour cream—which is non-beneficent and decidedly fattening, but tasty.

Breakfast Chicken

365 Breakfast Dishes, 1901

"Cut the chicken in pieces as for fricassee. Dip the pieces in beaten egg and then in fine bread crumbs. Season with pepper, salt and a very little fine sage (if you like the flavor). Put them in the dripping pan with bits of butter over them, and a little water in the pan. Bake slowly until they are done. Make a rich gravy in the dripping pan after the chicken is taken out."

For a quick rich gravy, mix 1 tsp yeast or meat extract with the drippings in the pan; add 1 tbsp wholewheat flour. Cook over a top burner for four to five minutes, gradually adding enough water or milk to make a creamy-textured sauce. Season if necessary.

Natural foods ingredients to serve four:

1 frying chicken, cut up	pepper
1 fertilized egg	small pinch sage
2 tbsp grated bread-	bits (about 1 tbsp) of
crumbs	butter or margarine
sea salt	a little water

You can add:

about 1 tbsp yogurt or sour cream to the gravy.

❧

Croquettes appeared often on nineteenth-century tables, probably to use up the vast quantities of left-overs, which must have been cooks' number-one head-ache in this age of magnificent eating.

Maria Parloa has some useful tips on making these little delicacies, which apply to all kinds of croquettes —including nut and fruit.

Croquettes

Miss Parloa's *New Cook Book*, 1880

"Care and practice are required for successfully making croquettes. The meat must be chopped fine, all the ingredients be thoroughly mixed, and the whole mixture be as moist as possible without spoiling the shape. Croquettes are formed in pear, round, and cylindrical shapes. The last is the best, as the croquettes can be moister in this form than in the two others.

"To shape: Take about a tablespoonful of the mixture, and with both hands, shape in the form of a cylinder. Handle as gently and carefully as if a tender bird. Pressure forces the particles apart, and thus breaks the form. Have a board sprinkled lightly with bread or cracker crumbs, and roll the croquettes *very gently* on this. Remember that the slightest pressure will break them. Let them lie on the board until all are finished, when, if any have become flattened, roll them into shape again. Cover a board *thickly* with crumbs. Have beaten eggs, slightly salted, in a deep plate. Hold a croquette in the left hand, and with a brush, or the right hand, cover it with the egg; then roll in the crumbs. Continue this until they are all crumbed. Place a few at a time in the frying basket (they should not touch each other), and plunge into boiling fat. Cook till a rich brown. It will take about a minute and a half. Take up, and lay on [a] paper [towel] in a warm pan."

These little chicken custards are equally good hot or cold. Any excess can be cut into pieces and tossed into a salad.

Boudins

365 Breakfast Dishes, 1901

"Heat 1 tablespoonful of butter in a saucepan, and add 2 tablespoonfuls of bread-crumbs and ½ a cupful of stock. Take this from the fire and add 1 pt. of finely chopped chicken meat, 1 tablespoonful of chopped parsley, a ¼ of a nutmeg grated, salt and pepper, and the yolks of 2 eggs slightly beaten. Mix thoroughly and pour into small cups. Half fill a baking pan with boiling water, set the cups in and bake 20 minutes. When done turn out on a hot platter and pour a cream (or arrowroot) sauce around."

Natural foods ingredients to serve four:

1 tbsp butter or margarine
2 tbsp grated bread-crumbs
½ c vegetable stock
1 pt (2 c) cooked chicken,* finely chopped

1 tbsp chopped parsley
¼ nutmeg, grated
sea salt
pepper
2 yolks of fertilized eggs
cream sauce (see CREAM SAUCE)

You can add:

minced parsley to cream sauce;
ARROWROOT SAUCE in place of cream.

---

* See PRESSED CHICKEN.

❧

You can adapt this recipe for nut, and of course, turkey, croquettes.

Wine Croquettes
(Chicken)

Table Talk, 1901

"Put ½ a cupful of rice into a [double] boiler and cook in 1½ cups water until soft and dry. Stir into this a tablespoonful of butter, then turn out on a dish to cool. Meanwhile, put the [cooked] minced chicken into a saucepan with ½ a cupful of water and season to taste. Into the cold rice beat 2 raw eggs and mix into the chicken when it (the chicken) is very hot, to which add a good tablespoonful of good sherry wine. Make into oblong rolls. Dip each in flour, then in beaten egg, and lastly in cracker dust. Fry to a golden brown and serve with a sauce made up of a wineglass full of sherry and a piece of butter the size of an egg [thickened with a little flour]. To this add finely chopped parsley and pour over the croquette."

To cool off the rice quickly: spread out thinly on a platter and leave for a few minutes in the refrigerator. The rice will then be cool enough not to cook the raw eggs on contact.

Natural foods ingredients to serve four:

½ c rice
1½ c water *plus* ½ c
1 tbsp butter or margarine *plus* 1 tbsp
2 eggs *plus* 1, beaten
2 c cooked minced chicken
1 good tbsp *plus* ½ c sherry

a little wholewheat flour
1 tsp or more vegetable extract
chopped parsley for garnish
cracker dust or breadcrumbs

That ugly-beautiful bird, the turkey, was erroneously thought to have come from—yes, Turkey. Actually, the bird was domesticated first by the Peruvians and then by the Mexicans, and finally by the North Americans.

Of all poultry except goose, turkey (surprisingly, because its meat is dry) has the most fat deposits; chicken the least.

Since you'll want an especially fine turkey for Thanksgiving dinner, be sure you choose one with the following characteristics: short neck, plump body with short, sharp claws, legs black and smooth—and it should, of course, be "organic."

In one of their recent, beautiful exhibitions (which incidentally you can see for free), entitled "Dining Out," the New York Public Library put on display the original "Instructions to Captain Woodleaf" proclaiming the feast of Thanksgiving, which was handed to him in 1619.

The recipe books on exhibit (all taken from the Research Libraries collection of 8,000 rare cookbooks) included such gems as Patrick Lamb's *Royal Cookery; or, The Complete Court-Cook* (1710) and Robert May's *The Accomplished Cook, or the Art and Mastery of Cookery* (1671).

In the courtly spirit of Patrick Lamb, the Thanksgiving turkey dinner Hugo Ziemann created for President Grover Cleveland must have been a splendid and festive meal. For a touch of such grandeur at your Thanksgiving table, cook a magnificent turkey, following this great chef's instructions, stuffing it with a mixture of oysters, breadcrumbs and herbs.

And like Mr. Ziemann, give thanks.

Roast Turkey

Hugo Ziemann and Mrs. Gillette's
White House Cook Book, 1887

". . . After washing, wipe the turkey dry, inside
and out, with a clean cloth, rub the inside with some
salt, then stuff the breast and body with 'Dressing
for Fowls.' Then sew up the turkey with a strong
thread, tie the legs and wings to the body, rub it over
with a little soft butter, sprinkle over some salt and
pepper, dredge with a little flour; place it in a dripping pan, pour in a cup of boiling water, and set it
in the oven. Baste the turkey often, turning it around
occasionally so that every part will be uniformly
baked. When pierced with a fork and the liquid runs
out perfectly clear, the bird is done. If any part is
likely to scorch, pin over it a piece of buttered white
paper. . . . Serve with cranberry sauce.

"*Gravy for Turkey:* When you put the turkey in
to roast, put the neck, heart, liver and gizzard into a
stewpan with a pint of water; boil until they become
quite tender; take them out of the water, chop the
heart and gizzard, mash the liver and throw away
the neck; return the chopped heart, gizzard and liver
to the liquor in which they were stewed; set it to one
side, and when the turkey is done it should be added
to the gravy that dripped from the turkey, having
first skimmed off the fat from the surface of the
dripping-pan; set it all over the fire, boil three minutes
and thicken with flour. . . . The garnishes for turkey
or chicken are fried oysters, thin slices of ham, slices
of lemon, fried sausages or forcemeat balls, also parsley."

Put the bird into a hot oven (400°), roast at this
temperature for twenty minutes, then reduce the heat
to about 325°; continue roasting at this temperature
until it is done. Test by inserting a knife or skewer.
Allow 25 minutes per pound cooking time.

Don't forget: Rub the oil thoroughly into the turkey; baste often.

Of the garnishes suggested, I prefer parsley; its dark green looks so pretty against the rich brown of the roasted bird.

Cook the gizzard, etc., for about 45 minutes, the liver for *five only*, then make the gravy as directed.

❧

Dressing or Stuffing for Fowls

Hugo Ziemann and Mrs. Gillette's
White House Cook Book, 1887

"For an eight or ten pound turkey, cut the brown crust from slices or pieces of stale bread until you have as much as the inside of a pound loaf; put it into a suitable dish, and pour tepid water (not warm, for that makes it heavy) over it; let it stand one minute, as it soaks very quickly. Now take up a handful at a time and squeeze it hard and dry with both hands, placing it, as you go along, in another dish; this process makes it very light. When all is pressed dry, toss it all up lightly through your fingers; now add pepper, salt—about a teaspoonful—also a teaspoonful of powdered summer savory, the same amount of sage, or the green herb [parsley] minced fine; add half a cup of melted butter, and a beaten egg, or not. Work thoroughly all together, and it is ready for dressing either fowls, fish or meats. A little chopped sausage in turkey dressing is considered by some an improvement, when well incorporated with the other ingredients. For geese and ducks, the stuffing may be made the same as for turkey with the addition of a few slices of onion chopped fine."

As a variation, add a small carrot, finely grated, together with one quarter or one half an apple, also finely grated. In place of crusts, use pieces of whole-wheat or wholegrain bread.

Natural foods ingredients to stuff an eight-to-ten-pound turkey:

pieces (about ¾ lb) wholegrain bread	1 tsp sea salt
1 c (about) lukewarm water	1 tsp summer savory
	1 tsp sage
pepper	½ c melted butter
	1 beaten egg

You can add:

oil in place of melted butter;
a little grated carrot and/or apple;
fines herbes in place of sage and savory.

Oyster Dressing or Stuffing

Hugo Ziemann and Mrs. Gillette's
White House Cook Book, 1887

"This is made with the same ingredients as the above,* with the exception of half a can of oysters drained, and slightly chopped and added to the rest. This is used mostly with boiled turkey and chicken, and the remainder of the can of oysters used to make an oyster sauce to be poured over the turkey when served; served generally in a separate dish, to be dipped out as a person desires.

---

* Use Mr. Ziemann's Dressing recipe (above) without variations.

"These recipes were obtained from an old colored cook, who was famous for his fine dressings for fowls, fish and meats, and his advice was *always* soak stale bread in *cold* liquid, either milk or water, when used for stuffing or for puddings, as they were much lighter. Hot liquid makes them heavy."

A useful tip.

❧

And Mrs. Gillette, ever the thoughtful housewife, gives this recipe for leftover turkey:

Turkey Scallop

Hugo Ziemann and Mrs. Gillette's
White House Cook Book, 1887

"Pick the meat from the bones of cold turkey, and chop it fine. Put a layer of bread-crumbs on the bottom of a buttered dish, moisten them with a little milk, then put in a layer of turkey with some of the filling [dressing], and cut small pieces of butter over the top; sprinkle with pepper and salt; then another layer of bread-crumbs, and so on until the dish is nearly full; add a little hot water to the gravy left from the turkey and pour over it; then take two eggs, two tablespoonfuls of milk, one of melted butter, a little salt and cracker-crumbs as much as will make it thick enough to spread on with a knife; put bits of butter over it, and cover. . . . Bake three-quarters of an hour [at 300°]. Ten minutes before serving, remove the [lid] and let it brown."

If you're out of dressing, scatter over a little of Francatelli's AROMATIC HERBACEOUS SEASONING for a fine zesty flavor.

Natural foods ingredients to serve four:

pieces (about 1 lb) cold turkey	pepper
	sea salt
1 cup grated breadcrumbs	a little hot water
2 tbsp milk *plus* 2 tbsp	leftover turkey gravy
1 cup leftover turkey dressing	2 eggs
	cracker crumbs
pieces (about 1½ tbsp) butter or margarine *plus* 1 tbsp melted	

You can add:

vegetable broth in place of gravy.

∾

If you're wondering what a "second joint" of turkey might be—it's the thigh, a word no lady of refinement at the turn of the century would think of saying. You can use thighs or legs in the following recipe.

Turkey Legs with Chestnut Puree

365 Breakfast Dishes, 1901

"Broil the second joints of the turkey, . . . (dipped in olive oil first). Make the following sauce: Put 1 pt. of shelled chestnuts into a pint of white soup stock; season with white pepper, salt, nutmeg, ½ teaspoonful of sugar and a small piece of butter; cover and cook slowly for ½ an hour. Press through a sieve [blend] and pour over the meat."

A tip for broiling and roasting turkey, both whole and in parts: with the fingers rub the oil into all the joints and over the skin.

Natural foods ingredients for four:

2 turkey legs or thighs.

For the Sauce:

1 pt (2 c) chestnuts, shelled	sea salt
1 pt (2 c) stock	a little grated nutmeg
pepper	½ tsp sugar
	small piece (1 tsp) butter

You can add:

oil in place of butter.

❧

Some Great, Oldfashioned Fish Dishes

STURGEON, cod, oysters, shrimp, sprats and smelts, carp, lobster, mackerel, pike and turbot, and other fish, all cooked in modern but age-old style, were popular in the good old days. Furthermore, Eliza Smith even pretties up her fish dishes with sauces featuring ingredients later made glorious by chefs like Francatelli, Escoffier, and Filippini: capers, ginger, horseradish, mace and cloves, and twists of lemon peel all go willy-nilly into Eliza's saucepan.

Today, in addition to the above, we serve flounder, haddock, halibut and pollock, and others, for there are no "new" fishes. Indeed, the list is too long to give here, and I'm sorry if I've omitted your favorite. But take heart: the basic methods for cooking fish are the same for all kinds.

Remember that fish is delicate, and must *never* be overcooked; treat all seafood with the same gentle touch you use for eggs and you won't fluff it. Fish, too, is best poached in water barely at boiling point. In baking, the dish should be checked for drying out.

But let the chefs and gourmet housewives of yesteryear tell you about seafood in their own words. Miss Shute, back in 1879, puts it right there:

Fish is Good

Miss Shute's *American Housewife*,
1879

"There is much nourishment in fish, little less than
in meat, weight for weight, and in effect it may be
more nourishing, considering how, from its softer
fibre, fish is more easily digested. Moreover, there is
in fish a substance which does not exist in the flesh
of land animals, namely, iodine, a substance which
may have a beneficial effect on the health. . . . If we
give attention to classes of people—classes as to the
quality of food they principally subsist on—we find
the class who subsist mostly on fish are especially
strong, healthy and prolific. In no class, except that
of fishers, do we see larger families, handsomer
women, more robust and active men. . . ."

Miss Shute is right. Fish *is* good good protein, and
in addition is rich in potassium, sodium, and phosphorus, and also sulphur acids. In fact, she errs only
by omission: it is *salt-water fish only* that is rich in
iodine, for obvious reasons. However, it is mostly
salt-water fish that we eat, particularly since river
pollution has made many people leary of eating fresh-
water fish, unless they're sure the waters in which the
fish were caught are pollution-free.

❧

Hugo Ziemann and Mrs. Gillette give two really great recipes for boiling and baking fish, the former an oldtimer from 1824.

Boiled White Fish

Hugo Ziemann and Mrs. Gillette's
White House Cook Book, 1887

" 'The most delicate mode of cooking white fish. Prepare the fish as for broiling, laying it open; put it into a dripping pan with the back down; nearly cover with water; to one fish two tablespoonfuls of salt; cover tightly and simmer (not boil) one-half hour. Dress with gravy [from the fish], a little butter and pepper, and garnish with hard-boiled eggs.'

"Taken from Mrs. A. W. Perry's Cook Book, Mackinac, 1824."

Follow Mrs. Perry's good advice to the letter, except in regard to the cooking time. Undoubtedly Mrs. P. boiled large fish whole; these require far longer cooking time than the cuts of cod, or whole flat fish such as flounder, that we serve today. Your timing, therefore, will probably vary from seven minutes or so (for fillets of sole) to fifteen, depending on the thickness of the fish.

For a change, cook white fish in milk, reserving the latter; when chilled it will form into a jelly with a delicate fishy flavor, which you can serve as is, in salad for instance. And smoked fish cooked in milk is exceptionally tasty.

∾

Baked White Fish
(Bordeaux Sauce)

Hugo Ziemann and Mrs. Gillette's
White House Cook Book, 1887

"Clean and stuff the fish. Put it in a baking pan
and add a liberal quantity of butter, previously rolled
in flour, to the fish. Put in the pan half a pint of
claret, and bake for an hour and a quarter. Remove
the fish and strain the gravy; add to the latter a gill
more of claret, a teaspoonful of brown flour and a
pinch of cayenne, and serve with the fish."

For a super stuffing, try Mrs. Rundell's recipe—one
of several in her *A New System of Domestic Management*—which she created for sewing into a gigantic
pike. But you bought halibut? No matter; her stuffing
is excellent inside any white fish.
Note: If you're baking fillets, alternate layers of fish
with stuffing; top with a layer of fish sprinkled with
breadcrumbs dotted with butter. Check for doneness
at fifty minutes.

Mrs. Rundell's Stuffing

adapted from *A New System of
Domestic Management,* 1806

Combine one cup grated wholegrain bread, a pinch
of *fines herbes,* two anchovies (or 1½ inch of anchovy
paste in a tube), 1 tbsp light oil or melted butter or
margarine, salt, pepper, a pinch of mace, 2 tbsp cream
or half-and-half, yolks of 2 eggs.
Put all the ingredients into the top half of a double
boiler. Stir; cook until mixture thickens.
For good measure, and a nineteenth century touch,
add a few oysters.

Chowder is the great American "social" dish, with good reason. Originally, chowders (from the French phrase *faire la chaudière*—literally "do the cauldron") were a hotch-potch mixture of fish flung into the *chaudière* by the fishermen of Brittany on return from the catch. Housewives added the tail ends of their good days' work—vegetables and other bits and pieces—and everyone dug in.

Here is Miss Shute's very American chowder:

Fish Chowder—Very Rich

Miss Shute's *American Housewife*,
1879

"Four tablespoonfuls of onion fried with pork, one quart of boiled potatoes mashed, one and a half pounds of ship's biscuits broken, one teaspoonful of thyme, one half bottle of tomato catsup; one bottle of port or claret; half a nutmeg grated, a few cloves, mace, allspice, and some slices of lemon; salt and some black pepper; six pounds of blue or white fish skinned and cut in slices, twenty-five oysters. First fry the pork, then put in the onions, and fry them a nice brown. Remove the kettle from the fire, skim out the bits of pork and onion, then put a layer of fish in the bottom of the kettle, salt, pepper and spices, then a layer of potato, oysters and biscuit with some of the wine and catsup; then another layer of fish and so on, having a layer of biscuit at the top; cover the whole with cold water, and let it boil fifteen or twenty minutes, or until the fish is done. Butter and milk may be used in place of the wine, if preferred; they should be put into the tureen and the chowder poured over it."

If your food philosophy is total meatlessness, omit the salt pork, and fry the onions in a flavorful oil like sesame. Add a tablespoonful yeast extract.

A word about ship's biscuits: these were hard, thick biscuits baked with coarse, unleavened flour and eaten by the crews of those beautiful sailing vessels built before the days of refrigeration.

For this chowder, any wholegrain, non-sweet cracker will do; alternatively serve with wholegrain pulled bread, broken into pieces. Crackers, however, are more authentic.

Natural foods ingredients sufficient for one ship's company:

4 tbsp chopped onion	½ nutmeg, grated
1 piece (about ½ lb) salt pork	a few cloves
	a little mace
1 qt (4 c) mashed potatoes	a little allspice
	slices of 2 lemons
1½ lb ship's biscuits, broken (see above)	sea salt
	black pepper
1 tsp thyme	6 lb blue or white fish, sliced
½ bottle tomato catsup	
1 bottle port or claret	25 oysters

You can add:

yeast extract in place of salt pork;
butter and milk in place of wine;
apple juice in place of wine;
pulled bread or crackers in place of ship's biscuits.

❧

Clams of all kinds are delicious, whether from the eastern seaboard or the Pacific coastline. The greatest in size and flavor, however, is the Giant Washington found on the Pacific coast, with the Hardshelled clam of the east tying neck and neck (or shell to shell).

Devilled Clams

365 Breakfast Dishes, 1901

"Drain 25 clams, pour a cupful of water over them to rinse them. [*Sauce:*] Scald 1 cupful of milk or cream, add 1 tablespoonful of butter and 2 of flour, stir until smooth and then add the raw yolks of 2 eggs, a tablespoonful of finely chopped parsley. Chop the clams and add them to the sauce. Fill small dishes or the clam shells with the mixture, cover with beaten egg and bread crumbs and brown in a hot oven."

Before draining, check the clams over. The shells should be tightly shut, indicating the occupants are alive inside. Scrub thoroughly and wash in several changes of water, then open up the shells by pouring boiling water over; let stand a few minutes. Then continue with the recipe.

Serve with lemon wedges.

Natural foods ingredients:

25 clams

For the sauce:

1 cup fresh milk or cream
1 tbsp butter or
   margarine
2 tbsp wholewheat flour
yolks of 2 eggs *plus* 1 egg

1 tbsp finely chopped
   parsley
breadcrumbs
sea salt to taste

❤

A cautionary word about soft-shelled crabs. These are actually hard-shelled crabs caught with their pants —or shells—down. Consequently, they are extremely delicate and perishable. Handle with care, and use at once.

Devilled Crabs

365 Breakfast Dishes, 1901

"Take the meat out of 12 boiled crabs, save the shells and wash them clean. Scald 1 cupful of milk and thicken with 2 tablespoonfuls of flour and 1 of butter. Take it from the fire and add the finely mashed yolks of 4 hard-boiled eggs, 1 tablespoonful of chopped parsley, cayenne pepper to taste and a pinch of salt; mix well, then add the crab meat. Fill the shells with this mixture; sprinkle crumbs on top and bits of butter. Bake until brown in a medium oven."

This can be made with canned crabmeat, and served in shells (scallop will do) or over buttered toast. The latter method of serving loses a certain charm, however, which surely is an important ingredient in this and every dish.

Natural foods ingredients to serve four:

12 boiled crabs, *or* 2 cans crabmeat
1 c fresh milk
2 tbsp wholewheat flour
1 tbsp butter or margarine *plus* bits

yolks of 4 hard-boiled eggs
1 tbsp parsley, chopped
pinch cayenne
sea salt to taste
breadcrumbs

You can add:

lemon wedges.

Hunters, in the wilds cooking their spoils in clay, usually wrapped the food in protective grasses first—according to one oldtime cookbook author. Here's how to cook in clay on home ground—in your kitchen.

Cooking Fish in Clay

Miss Shute's *American Housewife*, 1879

"Fish cooked in clay are said to be very delicious. The way you do it is as follows: After preparing, cover the fish with clay two inches thick, and put it into the fire. The clay hardens almost instantly, and the fish in its tough oven bakes through and through, retaining all its juices. The clay is then poked out of the fire, cooled with a dash of water, and a sharp stroke with a stick separates it from the fish. The fish's skin peels off with the clay, and the dish is ready. A little experience will enable one to cook a fish perfectly in this way. The clay is a good absorbant of the strong odors of the fish, and takes away all but the sweeter and best flavors."

This is truly cooking primitive style.

However, if you hesitate to wrap your family dinner in the local soil, you can buy pans made of clay imported from Italy under the brand name La Cotta, and sold in specialty shops. The pans are simple to use, and come complete with instructions.

Once you cook in clay, I assure you, you will do so again and again. And the dishes themselves, made of a beautiful, special terra cotta, grace the table in a simple manner no regular cookware can imitate.

❧

Without doubt, cod is the king of the inexpensive
ishes; it tastes good as steak, in fishcakes, broiled,
ried, or baked.

Codlings (baby cod) weigh about 3½ pounds,
vhile the big boys reach as much as 20 pounds. When
ouying a steak cut from the latter, be sure you get a
oiece cut from the "rump"—yes, fish have hiplines.
The tail end should, but usually doesn't, sell at a lower
orice, while the collar is the cheapest cut of all, still
elling for pennies per pound.

Cod Steaks à la Cardinal

Table Talk, 1901

"Have 3 lbs. of codfish cut into inch steaks and
sprinkle each slice well with salt, pepper and lemon
juice; brush them with melted butter; let stand for
10 minutes; then arrange in a large deep frying pan.
Pour over 1 cupful of fish stock and cover with
buttered paper; then with a closely fitting lid. Simmer
gently for 20 minutes; take up carefully with a skimmer and arrange on a hot platter. Mask each steak
with a spoonful of thick tomato sauce, which has
been slightly flavored with essence of anchovy, and
garnish with parsley and lemon."

Delicious; serve with FRANCATELLI'S TOMATO SAUCE.

Natural foods ingredients to serve four generously:

3 lb cod steaks	1 c tomato sauce (see
sea salt	FRANCATELLI'S
pepper	TOMATO SAUCE)
juice of 2 lemons	lemon wedges and parsley
1½ tbsp melted butter or	for garnish
margarine	
1 c fish stock (see FISH	
STOCK)	

∾

Dropped Codfish Balls

365 Breakfast Dishes, 1901

"One pint of raw fish, two pints of . . . potatoes, 2 eggs, butter the size of an egg, a little pepper. Pick up [chop] the fish very fine, measure lightly in a pint bowl; put the potatoes into the boiler; put the fish on top of them; boil half an hour; drain off all the water, and mash fish and potatoes together until very fine and light; add the butter, pepper and the egg well beaten. Have a deep kettle of boiling fat; take up a spoonful of the mixture, shape it carefully and drop into the hot fat; two minutes will brown it. Have the fat very hot and don't crowd the balls. Dip the spoon in the fat every time you take up a spoonful of the mixture."

Boil the fish and potatoes only till done—about twenty minutes. Choose small potatoes and cook unpeeled and well scrubbed in water to cover. Reserve the water—it's full of vitamins from the potatoes and flavor from the fish, and makes excellent fish stock.

If the kitty's low, buy inexpensive cod collar. (One collar, medium-sized, yields about 1½ pounds usable meat.)

Natural foods ingredients to serve four:

1 pt (2 c) raw fish, finely chopped
2 pt (2 lb) small potatoes
water to cover
butter or margarine the size of an egg (about 2 tbsp)

a little pepper
sea salt to taste
2 fertilized eggs, beaten
oil for frying

Codfish with Walnuts

Emma Telford's *Evening Telegram*
Cook Book, 1908

". . . pick apart one pound [cooked] codfish in as
large flakes as possible. Fry a pounded clove of garlic in
a tablespoonful of [oil] together with an onion cut
fine. Add the fish and fry a light brown. Have in readi-
ness four slices of bread soaked in cold water until soft
and then the moisture squeezed out. Add to the fish, together with a half cup of walnuts chopped fine. Stir
well, [season] add cream, or even water, to moisten,
cook five minutes and serve."

This ends up a creamy jumble. You can use buttermilk in place of cream; however, cod is not a fatty fish
and can take the amount of cream given in Emma's
recipe.

Natural foods ingredients to serve four:

1 lb fresh cod, cooked
1 clove garlic
1 tbsp oil
1 onion
4 slices wholegrain
   bread, soaked and
   squeezed

½ cup chopped walnut
   meats
cream or water (about
   ¼ cup)
sea salt

You can add:

lemon wedges;
goat or cow buttermilk in place of cream;
goat milk in place of cream.

❧

Here's an easy-to-make and an unusual supper dish, which you can fix in two sections—always a help when you're pressed for time. The oysters take few minutes to cook, the shortcake biscuit ten to fifteen.

Oyster Shortcake

Emma Telford's *Evening Telegram* Cook Book, 1908

"Make a good shortcake batter, using two cups pastry flour sifted with two teaspoonfuls baking powder and a half teaspoonful salt. Rub in a quarter cup butter, then add one egg beaten and mixed with a scant cup of milk. Spread on a buttered biscuit tin and bake in a quick oven. Split and spread with butter.

"For the filling, which should be ready by the time the cake is baked, scald a quart of oysters in their own liquor, skim, remove the oysters and put where they will keep hot. Strain the broth and return one cup to the saucepan. Mix together two tablespoonfuls butter and one of flour, stir into the boiling liquor and season with salt, pepper and celery salt. Let this just come to a boil, add three tablespoonfuls cream and the oysters. Stir a moment until well heated, fill into the shortcake and serve at once."

Cook the oyster and sauce mixture in a double boiler. To make the dish less rich, smother *un*buttered shortcake with mixture.

Natural foods ingredients to serve six to eight:

For the shortcake batter:

2 c wholewheat pastry flour	¼ c butter *plus* a little
2 tsp baking powder	1 fertilized egg
½ tsp sea salt	1 scant c fresh milk

For the filling:

1 qt (2 lb) oysters	sea salt
2 tbsp butter (or vegetable oil)	pepper
	celery salt to taste
1 tbsp wholewheat pastry flour	3 tbsp light cream

You can add:

buttermilk in place of cream.

Recipes for oysters abound in oldtime cookbooks, many in the gourmet class. This one can double as a sauce (go easy on the thickening) and comes from the household hints section of *Peterson's Magazine,* a periodical catering to the feminine world of the nineteenth century.

To Brown Oysters in Their Own Juice

Peterson's Magazine, 1858

"Take twenty-five oysters, and wash them in their own liquor. Then brown some butter in a frying-pan, dip the oysters in the broken yolk of an egg, and place them carefully in the pan not laying them one upon another; season them with pepper and salt. Brown the oysters nicely on both sides. Take them out of the pan, and pour into it their liquor, thickening it with a small portion of butter and flour; let it boil a short time, and then stir in the oysters carefully."

If cod is king, then salmon is undoubtedly emperor in the kitchen. Luscious—it's a fatty fish—and valuable as a food, salmon has significant amounts of calcium, phosphorus, and iodine, and of course no carbohydrates. And like cod, salmon is versatile.

You can bake, boil, and broil it; you can use it in kedgeree and croquettes, fish, cakes, patties, and pie; you can fry, sauté, and barbecue its delicious steaks; you can serve it cold, unadorned but for lemon wedges; you can casserole, curry, and cream it—the list is virtually endless. Come to think of it, you can even substitute cod.

The next two recipes are typical; the first uses expensive smoked salmon, the second the cheapest, tail-end cut. Both are excellent.

Broiled Salmon (Smoked)

365 Breakfast Dishes, 1901

"Into a pan of cold water put 1 lb. of smoked salmon; let it boil up; then drain and rinse off with cold water. Wipe the salmon dry and brush over with melted butter. Broil carefully for 5 minutes. Make a sauce for this with 1 tablespoonful of melted butter, juice of ½ a lemon, salt and pepper, and a teaspoonful of chopped parsley. Pour over the fish and serve."

Fillets of Salmon à l'Indienne

Francatelli's *Cook's Guide*, 1888

"Procure a pound and a half of salmon from the tail end (that part being cheaper); divide the fish from the backbone by running or slipping the edge of the knife along the side of the spine; and when this is effected, remove the skin in like manner; cut the fish into neat squares or heart-shaped pieces, about a quarter of an inch thick; dip these fillets in some beaten egg; drain and roll them in some fine breadcrumbs; fry them of a light-fawn color in some [oil] previously made very hot for the purpose; and when done, dish them up neatly and pour over them some Indian Sauce and sprinkle over the fillets some finely shred peel of the green mountain gherkins."

For "green mountain" read "health store."

To flour and season fish and other items in minimal time: put 1 tbsp of flour per serving into a paper or plastic bag, add salt, pepper, and other seasoning if any. Shake to mix thoroughly; add fish (or what have you). Grasp the closed top of the bag firmly and shake again violently. After a few seconds of this treatment, you'll find on opening up the bag that its contents will be nicely floured and seasoned ready for the pan.

Natural foods ingredients to serve six:

1½ lb salmon pieces or tail ends	peel of 3 or 4 gherkins (small cucumbers)
1 egg, beaten	sea salt
breadcrumbs	pepper
oil for frying	

❧

As you may know, there's no breed of fish called "sardine."

Actually, "sardine" is used to describe a number of small fish of the herring family. The name comes of course from Sardinia, and was given to the little pilchards fished off the coast of that beautiful island.

You can buy cans of sardines (imported from Norway and the Mediterranean, or culled locally off the coasts of Maine and California) packed in tomato paste, mustard, or olive or soybean oil. There's an enormous difference in quality, price and flavor between brands, and as always you should shop around until you find the one you like best—which may not be the most expensive.

Sardine Sauté

365 Breakfast Dishes, 1901

"Drain the fish free from oil. Fry them quickly in melted butter. Dust with paprika and squeeze a little lemon juice over them. Heap [hot] mashed browned potatoes into a mound on a round platter; lay the fish up against the sides, tails up, and garnish with lemon and parsley."

◆◇

The scallop, one of the crowning glories in *haute cuisine*, abounds along the Eastern seaboard, as far down as the Hatteras. Actually, only the great muscle or heart of the bivalve reaches the kitchen. The rest is discarded as inedible.

Scallops, like all shellfish, respond to tender treatment. When cooking (scalding), keep the temperature at barely boiling, and when browning, remove from the oven sooner rather than later.

Baked Scallops

Table Talk, 1901

"Scald the scallops for five minutes and drain. Cook 1 tablespoonful of chopped onion in 1 tablespoonful of butter until tender, add ½ of a cupful of chopped mushrooms and cook until all begin to color; then add 1 pt. of cream sauce, the drained scallops (1 qt.) and a high seasoning of salt and pepper. Turn into a shallow baking dish, sprinkle with crumbs (which have been browned in a little butter) and place in a hot oven for ten minutes."

Natural foods ingredients to serve four:

2 lb scallops (1 qt)   1 pt (2 c) CREAM SAUCE
1 tbsp chopped onion   sea salt
1 tbsp butter or   pepper
   margarine *plus* a little   toasted breadcrumbs
½ c chopped mushrooms

You can add:

arrowroot sauce in place of Cream Sauce.

Miss Shute is emphatic on the subject of cooking scallops:

Scallops

Miss Shute's *American Housewife,*
1879

"These are best fried. Dip them into egg and crumbs; fry them in hot [oil] quickly; skim them out of the [oil]; put them into a collander and keep them hot until all are fried."

Mackerel, of which Spanish is but one variety of some sixty, is a truly delectable fish, beautiful to behold in its blue and black skin, which has a satiny shine when fresh.

Cautionary note: Never buy flaccid, dull-looking mackerel. This is a hobo fish, risky to bite into unless truly fresh.

Broiled Spanish Mackerel

Hugo Ziemann and Mrs. Gillette's
White House Cook Book, 1887

"Split the fish down the back, take out the backbone, wash it in cold water, dry it with a clean, dry cloth, sprinkle it lightly with salt and lay it on a buttered gridiron, over a clear fire, with the flesh side downward, until it begins to brown; then turn over the other side. Have ready a mixture of two tablespoonfuls of butter melted, a tablespoonful of lemon juice, a teaspoonful of salt, some pepper. Dish up the fish hot from the gridiron on a hot dish, turn over the mixture and serve it while hot."

Serve with GOOSEBERRY SAUCE, omitting the lemon juice. Absolutely great.

The delicate-flavored sole, or dab, swims around off the Atlantic coast.

It's a non-fatty fish, similar to flounder, so don't be alarmed at Mrs. Rundell's generous helping of cream; sole can take the added richness, and so can oysters. In fact, her method is far more imaginative, if richer, than the ordinary poaching job, slathered in white sauce, which is usually the lot of the expensive sole.

Indeed, recipes like the two that follow show how many nuances in cooking have been lost through the years.

Soles

Mrs. Rundell's *Domestic Management*,
1806

"Take two or three soles, divide them from the backbone, and take off the head, fins and tail. Sprinkle the insides with salt, roll them up tight from the tail end upwards, and fasten with small skewers [toothpicks]. If large or middling, put half a fish in each roll; small do not answer. Dip them into yolks of eggs, and cover them with crumbs. Do the egg over them again, and then put more crumbs; and fry them a beautiful color in [oil], or for fastday in clarified butter.

Mix a sprinkling of sesame seeds, roasted of course, with the breadcrumbs. Allow one fillet per person. Serve with lemon wedges.

Natural foods ingredients to serve four to six:

2 to 3 sole (4 to 6 fillets)   breadcrumbs
sea salt   oil or clarified butter for
yolks of 2 eggs   frying

You can add:

roasted sesame seeds;
lemon wedges.

Sole Pie

Mrs. Rundell's *Domestic Management*,
1806

"Split some soles from the bone and cut the fins close; season with a mixture of salt, pepper, a little nutmeg and pounded mace, and put them in layers with oysters. They eat excellently. A pair of middling sized ones will do, and half a hundred of oysters. Put in the dish the oyster-liquor, two or three spoonfuls of broth, and some butter. When the pie comes home, pour in a cupful of thick cream."

Housewives in Greece traditionally put out part of their baking chores, and possibly Mrs. Rundell did too, back in the early 1800s when servants often lived in cottages on the edge of the estates where they worked. Certainly, Mrs. Rundell's pie was baked away from her house—how else to account for its "home-coming"?

Your pie, baked safely in your kitchen, can have its cup of thick cream (or better still, yogurt) duly warmed and poured over just before serving.

For a Charleston-style pie, sans crust, sprinkle with toasted breadcrumbs dotted with butter, and bake in a moderate oven (350–375°) for about 45 minutes, at which time check for doneness.

Natural foods ingredients to serve six to eight:

fillets of 3 or 4 soles	2 or 3 tbsp broth (See
sea salt	STOCK)
pepper	a little butter (about
a little nutmeg	1 tbsp)
a little ground mace	1 c heavy cream
50 oysters	

You can add:

vegetable extract and water in place of broth;
yogurt in place of heavy cream.

❧

Whitebait are minute fish caught in fine nets, together with all kinds of fishy oddities which of course are removed at once, on landing. Nevertheless, whitebait should be picked over carefully, just in case.

These delicate little fish are found in both salt and fresh water, and keep their silvery company in enormous shoals. Like the sardine, there are many varieties, all looking alike.

Devilled Whitebait

Table Talk, 1901

"Wash the fish through two waters, drain thoroughly and dry them on a soft cloth. Have ready a second cloth well floured. Drop the fish on this and roll them over and over until they are well and evenly floured. Transfer them to a wire frying-basket and plunge into smoking hot fat. When a pale golden color (which will take about 2 minutes), drain them, sprinkle with salt and cayenne or paprika and serve on a napkin."

Incidentally, don't chop off the heads and tails. Whitebait are munched whole, as is.

⊸≡{ 4 }≡⊸

Lighter Dishes with Eggs and Cheese, and Some with Beans and Rice

To make a thick Cream-Cheese.

TAKE the Morning's Milk from the Cow, and the Cream of the Night's Milk and Runnet, pretty cool together, and when 'tis come, make it pretty much in the Cheese-fat, and in a little Salt, and make the Cheese thick in a deep Mold, or a Melon Mold if you have one: keep it a Year and half, or two Years before you cut it: It must be well salted on the outside.

To make a Slip-coat Cheese.

TAKE new Milk and Runnet, quite cold, and when 'tis come, break it as little as you can in putting it into the Cheese-fat, and let it stand and whey itself for some time; then cover it, and set about two pound weight on it, and when it will hold together, turn it out of that Cheese-fat, and keep it turning upon clean Cheese-fats for two or three days, till it has done wetting, and then lay it on sharp-pointed Dock-leaves till 'tis ripe: Shift the Leaves often.

Eliza Smith's *The Compleat Housewife*, 1727

Oldtime Egg Dishes—from Barnyard Hens

HOMEMAKERS of the good old days, like Eliza Smith and her American cousins, had all aspects of housewifery at their capable fingertips. At this period—late eighteenth and early nineteenth centuries—all wives, both rich and unpretentious, oversaw flocks of servants and/or farmhands at work as in a factory.

The role of production manager—which is what these oldtime housewives virtually held—was no sinecure; farmers' wives took turn at every job from cheese-making to mixing ink for quill pens (a kitchen chore in those days). The sophisticated in Eliza's home country rented dairy farms so that the lady of the house could supervise the making of the rich butters and cheese; sometimes she even took turns at churning, so highly did she rate her dairy products.

How right these women were: eggs and cheese are two of the most nourishing forms of protein.

Somewhere along the decades we've lost this sense of the personal importance of food; we've let the manufacturer take over. With vegetables in cans, and cheese sunken in wax covers in place of porous cheesecloth (which allows the cheese to "breathe") comes the cartoned egg no Eliza Smith or Amelia Simmons would glance at—so pallid are its devitalized yolk and flavor. Laid by cooped, production-line hens, the modern egg lacks the germ of life, being lackluster because unfertilized.

Most natural-foods cooks buy their fertilized eggs, with their rich yellow yolks, at the local health stores, paying higher prices for this natural product of organically-fed barnyard hens. Yet there's good reason for these higher prices: the hens who lay these eggs are fertilized by their roosters—a happenstance the cooped-up hen does not experience, poor thing, on the production line that keeps costs to a minimum.

Hens are great personalities, as anyone who's been on friendly terms with these birds will tell you. Helen, a small bantam and a close friend when I was eight, had the sparkling eye and bright beak of the happy, free-roving, barnyard hen. Her little nodding head expressing motherly approval, she would follow me around the farmyard, trailed by a flock of other fussy hen-types, and a quartet of squawking geese. Each morning I would seek—and find—the rich, golden-yolked egg she'd laid just for me (of course).

As you can see, there's greater flavor and nutrition in the eggs laid in some mossy place by the hen fed organic dinners (plus the goodies she digs out of the ground with her sharp little claws) and duly fertilized by the local Casanova, than in those produced by the bored spinster in her claustrophobic coop. These latter are pale in comparison, literally.

The fertilized eggs you buy in your local health store (often guaranteed, incidentally, because it's virtually impossible for a layman to recognize a fertilized egg) are similar to those used years ago in the recipes that follow, including of course Mrs. Beeton's recipe for Soufflé.

∾

Mrs. Beeton's instructions are about the clearest and most helpful I've ever read. So if you've lost heart because your soufflés faint going from oven to table, or you balked at the horrendous task, read on and digest Mrs. Beeton's good advice. Your courage, like your soufflé, will rise heavenwards.

To Make a Soufflé

Mrs. Beeton's *Household Management*, 1861

"*Ingredients*—3 heaped tablespoonfuls of potato-flour, rice-flour, arrowroot, or tapioca, 1 pint of milk, 5 eggs, a piece of butter the size of a walnut, sifted sugar to taste, ¼ saltspoonful of salt, flavouring.

"*Mode*—Mix the potato-flour, or whichever is used, with a little of the milk; put it into a saucepan, with the remainder of the milk, the butter, salt, and sufficient pounded sugar to sweeten the whole nicely. Stir these ingredients over the fire until the mixture thickens; then take it off the fire, and let it cool a little. Separate the whites from the yolks of the eggs, beat the latter and stir them into the soufflé batter. Now whisk the whites of the eggs to the firmest possible froth, for on this depends the excellence of the dish; stir them to the other ingredients, and add a few drops of essence of any flavouring that may be preferred; such as vanilla, lemon, orange, ginger, etc., etc. Pour the batter into a soufflé-dish, put it immediately into the oven, and bake for about ½ hour; then take it out, put the dish into another, more ornamental one, such as is made for the purpose; hold a salamander or hot shovel (hot saucepan lid) over the soufflé; strew it with sifted sugar, and send it instantly to the table. The secret of making a soufflé well is to have the eggs well whisked [beaten], but particularly the whites, the oven not too hot, and to send it to the table the moment it comes from the oven. If the soufflé be ever so well made, and it is allowed to stand before being sent to the table, its

appearance and goodness will be entirely spoiled.
Soufflés may be flavoured in various ways, but must
be named accordingly. Vanilla is one of the most
delicate and recherché flavourings that can be used for
this very fashionable dish.

"*Time*—About ½ hour in the oven; 2 or 3
minutes to hold the salamander over.

"*Average cost* is 1s. Sufficient for 3 or 4 persons.
Seasonable at any time."

❧

Surprisingly, many cooks don't know how to boil an
egg. Actually, the well-boiled egg is not boiled, but
coddled. So follow the instructions below, cooking
your breakfast egg at the lowest simmer, i.e., just below boiling point. And throw out the egg timer.

Boiled Eggs

365 Breakfast Dishes, 1901

"Have a large saucepan containing boiling water.
Put into it the number of eggs desired. Put the saucepan on the back of the stove where the water will not
boil. Cook eight minutes if desired soft boiled, forty
if hard boiled. These are delicious."

The stove is the oldtime kitchen range, of course,
which burnt wood. As we mentioned earlier, the heat
varied according to the distance the pot was placed
from the fire beneath. Back of the stove, which is mentioned in several recipes, was farthest from the heat;
any pot placed there simmered rather than boiled.

❧

Hints on Cooking Eggs

Remember:

Gently does it—cook eggs slowly.

One medium-sized egg weighs about 1¾ ounces.

One dozen eggs weighs about 1¼ to 1½ pounds.

Don't wash eggs until ready for use; washing removes the protective coating which stops germs from attacking the innards.

Don't cook eggs in a lightweight pan which heats up quickly; the eggs will cook too fast, too soon.

Use a piece of eggshell to remove traces of yolks which sometimes spread into the whites when the eggs are broken.

In proportion to their small size, eggs are very satisfying. So keep track of the number you serve; a huge omelet can be as stifling (and as acid-forming) as a one-pound steak.

Leftover egg yolks can be poached, then slivered or crumbled into sauces or curries, etc.

Hard-boiled eggs will not spin; uncooked ones will. A good test if you need to figure out which is which.

To stop poached eggs from spreading, stir in one direction only.

To keep scrambled eggs from drying out, cook in a double boiler. Alternatively, if serving a large batch, save one egg uncooked but beaten, and stir it into the finished mess—the warmth of the cooked eggs will cook the newly added egg just enough.

Use sour milk when possible for mixing omelets and scrambled eggs; it "lifts" the mixture and gives a delicate, off-beat flavor.

When frying or scrambling eggs, remember to remove from the fire while still moist. Otherwise, they'll continue cooking in the hot pan.

Use an egg cutter or well-sharpened knife to slice hard-boiled eggs. If they tend to break, give up and serve them crumbled instead of sliced.

Chop up cooked egg whites (from hard-boiled egg yolks) for use as garnish.

❧

These Egg Cutlets, piled on a pretty platter, look important—and mouth-watering, particularly when dotted with sprigs of parsley. Make ahead of time, and serve as a Main-Dish-in-a-Hurry.

Egg Cutlets

365 Breakfast Dishes, 1901

"Put 6 eggs in a saucepan; cover with cold water and simmer for an hour. Scald 1 pt. of milk in a double boiler; rub together to a paste 2 tablespoonfuls of butter and 4 of flour; turn this into the scalded milk and stir slowly until it dissolves and thickens. Cover and cook 5 minutes, then season with 1 teaspoonful of salt, ½ of a teaspoonful of paprika, a dash of cayenne, 1 teaspoonful of onion juice and a pinch of mace. Take from the fire, add the hard-boiled eggs, chopped rather coarsely, and 1 tablespoonful of chopped parsley. Spread out on a buttered dish and set away to cool. Dust the hands lightly with flour and shape spoonfuls of the mixture in small cutlets, being careful to pat them out until of an even thickness; use as little flour as possible, or the creamy consistency will be lost. When all are shaped, dip each cutlet into slightly beaten egg, then in fine dried bread crumbs, and immerse in smoking hot fat until golden brown. Drain on unglazed paper and serve with tomato or cream sauce."

For hints on how to boil an egg slowly and beautifully, see BOILED EGGS.

Natural foods ingredients to serve six:

6 fertilized eggs *plus*
1 beaten
1 pt (2 c) milk
2 tbsp butter or
margarine
4 tbsp wholewheat
flour *plus* a little
1 tsp sea salt
½ tsp paprika

dash of cayenne
1 tsp onion juice
pinch of mace
1 tbsp chopped parsley
½ c fine dried bread-
crumbs
butter or oil for frying
TOMATO SAUCE *or* CREAM
SAUCE

You can add:

yogurt or sour cream in place of sauce;
a little sesame or sunflower meal to the dried breadcrumbs.

❧

Creamed Eggs

365 Breakfast Dishes, 1901

"Take the shell off of hard-boiled eggs, cut them
in half, stand them on rounds of toasted bread. Cap
each egg with a mushroom previously cooked in a
little butter. Pour a cream sauce around and serve."

Natural foods ingredients to serve four:

4 hard-boiled eggs
4 slices wholegrain toast
butter (*or* oil) for frying

4 mushrooms
CREAM SAUCE

You can add:

chopped parsley and/or toasted sesame seeds sprinkled over the cream sauce.

❧

Easy to make once you get the knack, quick to the table (to use oldtime parlance), and invariably delicious, omelets are the ideal show-off dish. Below, Mrs. Gillette and Hugo Ziemann toss off their best with easy-to-follow directions which include a few hints not found in most cookbooks.

Omelets

Hugo Ziemann and Mrs. Gillette's
White House Cook Book, 1887

"In making an omelet, care should be taken that the omelet pan is hot and dry. To ensure this, put a small quantity of lard or suet [or olive oil] into a clean frying-pan, let it simmer a few minutes, then remove it; wipe the pan dry with a towel, and then put in a tablespoonful of butter. The smoothness of the pan is most essential, as the least particle of roughness will cause the omelet to stick. As a general rule, a small omelet can be made more successfully than a large one, it being much better to make two small ones of four eggs each, than to try doubleing the number of eggs in one omelet and fail.* Allow one egg to a person in making an omelet and one tablespoonful of milk; this makes an omelet more puffy and tender than one made without milk. Many prefer them without milk.

"Omelets are called by the name of what is added to give them flavor, as minced ham, salmon, onions, oysters, etc., beaten up in the eggs in due quantity, which gives as many different kinds of omelets.

"They are also served over many kinds of thick sauces or purées, such as tomatoes, spinach, endive, lettuce, celery, etc.

* See "Trio of Omelets" in my *200 Really Great Natural Foods, Recipes*, Ballantine, 1972. —B-M. P.

"If vegetables are to be added, they should be already cooked, seasoned and hot; place in the centre of the omelet, just before turning; so with mushroom, shrimps, or any cooked ingredients. All omelets should be served the moment they are done, as they harden by standing, and care taken that they do not *cook too much.*

"Sweet omelets are generally used for breakfast or plain desserts."

For an easy-to-fix, delicious sweet omelet: Fill Mrs. Gillette's Plain Omelet (below) with whole-fruit strawberry preserve. (Omit the pepper, and go easy on the salt, of course.)

Plain Omelet

Hugo Ziemann and Mrs. Gillette's
White House Cook Book, 1887

"Put a smooth, clean, iron frying-pan on the fire to heat; meanwhile, beat four eggs, very light, the whites to a stiff froth, and the yolks to a thick batter. Add to the yolks four tablespoonfuls of milk, pepper and salt; and lastly stir in the whites lightly. Put a piece of butter nearly half the size of an egg into the heated pan; turn it so that it will moisten the entire bottom, taking care that it does not scorch. Just as it begins to boil, pour in the eggs. Hold the frying pan handle in your left hand, and, as the eggs whiten, carefully, with a spoon, draw up lightly from the bottom, letting the raw part run out on the pan, till all be equally cooked; shake with your left hand, till the omelet be free from the pan, then turn with a spoon one half of the omelet over the other; let it remain a moment, but continue shaking, lest it ad-

here; toss to a warm platter held in the right hand, or
lift with a flat, broad shovel; the omelet will be firm
around the edge, but creamy and light inside."

Good advice if you don't own a double-sided omelet
pan.

Meat or Fish Omelet

Hugo Ziemann and Mrs. Gillette's
White House Cook Book, 1887

"Take cold meat, fish, game or poultry of any
kind; remove all skin, sinew, etc. and either cut it
small or pound it to a paste in a mortar, together
with a proper proportion of spices and salt; then
either toss it in a buttered frying-pan over a clear fire
till it begins to brown, and pour beaten eggs upon it,
or beat it up with the eggs, or spread it upon them
after they have begun to set in the pan. In any case
serve hot, with or without a sauce; but garnished
with crisp herbs in branches, pickles, or sliced lemon.
The right proportion is one tablespoonful of meat to
four eggs. A little milk, gravy, water, or white wine,
may be advantageously added to the eggs while they
are being beaten."

For an extra-good Cheese Omelet, and other egg-
and-cheese dishes, see Cheese Dishes.

Omelet of Herbs

Hugo Ziemann and Mrs. Gillette's
White House Cook Book, 1887

"Parsley, thyme, and sweet marjoram mixed gives the famous *omelette aux fines herbes* so popular at every wayside inn in the most remote corner of sunny France. An omelet 'jardiniere' is two tablespoonfuls of mixed parsley, onion, chives, shalots, and a few leaves each of sorrel and chervil, minced fine and stirred into the beaten eggs before cooking. It will take a little more butter to fry it than a plain one."

For Francatelli, a poet at heart, the butter "fritters," and his golden omelet rests on the plate like a beautiful, Victorian cushion.

What more could a hen ask for her egg?

Omelet with Fine-Herbs

Francatelli's *Cook's Guide*, 1888

"Break three eggs in a basin; to these add a spoonful of cream, a small pat of butter broken in small pieces, a little chopped parsley and shalot, some pepper and salt; then put two ounces of fresh butter in an omelet-pan on the stove-fire. While the butter is melting, whip the eggs, etc., well together until they become frothy; as soon as the butter begins to fritter, pour the eggs into the pan, and stir the omelet; as the eggs appear to set, and become firm, roll the omelet into the form of an oval cushion; allow it to acquire a golden colour on one side over the fire, and then turn it out on its dish; pour a little thin sauce . . . under it, and serve."

A super omelet—don't skip one step, or reduce the butter or cream.

Heat up a little TOMATO SAUCE, adding water if necessary, and trickle under the omelet before serving.

Natural foods ingredients for one large omelet:

3 fertilized eggs
1 tbsp cream
1 small pat (2 tsp) butter
 plus 2 oz (2 tbsp)
a little (2 tsp) chopped
 parsley
a little (1 tsp) chopped
 shallot (or to taste)
pepper
sea salt
a little sauce (e.g.,
 TOMATO SAUCE)

That Escoffier-style gesture—setting a blaze shooting up from your pièce de résistance—will make you a chef-de-luxe.

This omelet (in its convict stripes typical of the ornamented desserts ogled by those bearded gourmets of a century ago) goes up in magnificent, eerie-blue flames.

Rum Omelet

The Cook, circa 1890

"Break three eggs separately; put them into a bowl and whisk them thoroughly with a fork. The longer they are beaten, the lighter will the omelet be. Beat up a teaspoonful of milk with the eggs and continue to beat until the last moment before pouring into the pan, which should be over a hot fire. As soon as the omelet sets, remove the pan from the hottest part of the fire. Slip a knife under it to prevent sticking to the pan. When the centre is almost firm, slant the pan, work the omelet in shape to fold easily and neatly, and when slightly browned, hold a platter against the edge of the pan and deftly turn it out on to the hot dish. Dust a liberal quantity of powered sugar over it, and singe the sugar into neat stripes with a hot iron rod, heated in the coals; pour a [wine] glass of warm Jamaica rum around it, and when it is placed on the table set fire to the rum. With a tablespoon dash the burning rum over the omelet, put out the fire and serve."

To get the brown-and-white strip effect, you will need to use white sugar—surely for once permissible.

Use a shashlik rod, or oldfashioned metal skewer, as your "painting" tool.

Natural foods ingredients for one large omelet:

3 fertilized eggs
1 tsp milk
pinch sea salt
1 tbsp powdered sugar
  (about)

1 wineglass (¼ c)
  warm rum

❧

Here's a simple version of an old favorite:

Curried Eggs

365 Breakfast Dishes, 1901

"Cut 6 hard-boiled eggs in slices; make a curry sauce with 2 tablespoonfuls of butter and 2 of flour, 1 oz. of curry powder; stir until the flour is cooked; then add 1 cupful of stock; let it come to a boil. Put into it the slices of egg, and pour all over rounds of toasted bread."

Natural foods ingredients to serve six:

6 fertilized hard-boiled eggs

For the sauce:

2 tbsp butter or
  margarine
2 tbsp wholewheat flour
1 oz (1 tbsp) CURRY
  POWDER

1 c vegetable stock
6 slices wholegrain bread,
  toasted

You can add:

yeast extract and water in place of stock.

Serving slices of plain bread alongside egg dishes was too humdrum for nineteenth century housewife-chefs. In the manner of their era, these charming ladies decorated everything they could grasp from cupcakes to cushions—to kids, for whom they embroidered beautiful bonnets and shawls, and underwear like their own. Even horses were affectionately decked in their handiwork—in crocheted lace caps, with bunny-like ear-pieces.

In these two recipes for Eggs and Bread Sauce, bread is used deliciously and decoratively; try these ideas for a fancy breakfast, brunch, or supper.

Eggs with Bread Sauce

Table Talk, 1901

"Put 1 heaping cupful of bread crumbs (the centre of the bread) into a saucepan with a cupful and a half of milk, ½ a teaspoonful of salt, a dash of cayenne and ½ a teaspoonful of onion juice and simmer slowly until thick and smooth, beating several times with a spoon. Pour the sauce into a broad shallow dish and break carefully over it ½ a dozen eggs. Place in a hot oven until the eggs are set, then send quickly to the table."

Natural foods ingredients to serve six:

6 fertilized eggs

For the bread sauce:

1 heaping c wholegrain breadcrumbs, fresh	dash of cayenne
1½ c milk	½ tsp onion juice (or more, to taste)
½ tsp sea salt	

You can vary these recipes by using different wholegrain breads. Six-grain, oat, or corn bread can all be used for a change of pace; however, wholegrain rye is tricky because of its heavier texture.

Eggs in Bread Sauce

Table Talk, 1901

"Slice 1 good-sized onion, cover with boiling water and let stand 5 minutes. Drain, add 1 pt. of milk, 2 cloves, ½ a blade of mace and ¼ of a teaspoonful of salt and simmer for ½ an hour. Rub through a sieve, pressing through as much of the pulp as possible [or blend]. Into a saucepan put 1 heaping tablespoonful of butter and flour. Set over the fire and when melted and mixed add the milk and onion and stir until smooth and thickened. Now add ½ a cupful of stale bread crumbs and salt and pepper to taste. Simmer for five minutes and turn into a buttered baking dish. Drop in carefully 5 eggs and place in a hot oven until the eggs are set."

Natural foods ingredients to serve five:

5 fertilized eggs

For the bread sauce:

1 large onion	1½ tbsp butter or
about 2 c boiling water	margarine
1 pt (2 c) milk	1½ tbsp wholegrain flour
2 cloves	½ cup wholegrain
½ blade (pinch)	breadcrumbs
powdered mace	pepper
¼ tsp sea salt *plus* to	
taste	

❧

And finally, something to delight the kids. For real surprise boxes, fry extra slices of bread separately. Place one on top of each box to make a lid.

Eggs in Boxes

365 Breakfast Dishes, 1901

"Cut slices of bread 1½ inch thick, trim them off neatly and scoop out the centers to make a box. Dip them in beaten egg and fry them in hot fat until a light brown. Drain on . . . paper towel. Into each of these boxes drop an egg, dust lightly with salt [and pepper] and cook them in the oven for 2 or 3 minutes."

Natural foods ingredients to serve four:

4 thick slices wholegrain   4 fertilized eggs
  bread   sea salt
2 fertilized eggs, beaten   pepper
oil for frying

You can add:

lids to the boxes; see above.

Cheese Dishes—Nutritious, Delicious, and Filling

~~~~~~

THERE'S no sight more welcoming than a huge globe of cheese set upright on the cheeseboard. If you've never served cheese, whole, in this manner—well, it's worth organizing a party around the cheese, which can weigh several pounds and fill up a lot of guests.

Actually, cheese served in any manner is extremely nourishing, so use it sparingly, advice cheese-lovers often ignore. Gourmets today, like their banqueting counterparts of the last century, often end a hefty meal picking their way across the cheeseboard.

In the old days, the lady of the house made her own cheese, and probably served no other. Today, although we have over four hundred varieties to choose from, most natural-foods cooks settle first for goat's-milk cheese, and Roquefort, which is made with ewe's milk. You can use the former in the recipes that follow, while Roquefort of course gives a pleasantly sharp flavor to salad dressing, and can be used crumbled into sauces or over vegetables and salads, as is.

Eliza Smith gives directions for making her own full-bodied cheeses, and they're certainly complicated. However, you can make excellent cheese by adopting the far simpler method of dripping off the whey from sour milk, the basic premise of all cheese-making.

Let a pint of milk curdle: the solid mass now formed is made up of curds and whey. When you separate the two, the curds (or milk solids) become a thick mass (the cheese) while the liquid drains off, and becomes whey.

An easy method of separating is to hang a muslin bag from the kitchen faucet, with a bowl sitting directly beneath. Pour the sour milk into the muslin bag; leave several hours, during which time the whey will ease through the muslin and drop into the bowl. Incidentally, a white nylon stocking cut off short makes an efficient cheese bag.

Add salt and flavoring to the thick curd, or cheese, softening it by beating with a fork, and adding a little whey if necessary.

Don't on any account throw out the whey. Use in place of milk in egg dishes, in biscuits, crackers, cakes, and breads. Not only do baked goodies cook lighter with whey, but it imparts a subtle sharp flavor. It can be the making of a plain muffin, lifting it right out of its humble station. In fact, if you read the list of ingredients on expensive packets of cookies, you'll see whey, and its rich cousin sour cream, lined up over and over.

Cheese is not an easy food to cook, though its use in recipes seems simple enough. But it's apt to toughen if badly treated, taking revenge by sitting indigestibly on delicate stomachs.

Queen Victoria's Francatelli has some practical hints for making that deceptively simple standby, toasted cheese.

Toasted Cheese

Francatelli's Cook's Guide, 1888

"Cheddar is allowed to be the richest cheese, and is therefore the best adapted for toasting, from the fact that it is not so liable as other cheese to become tough and uneatable before it is cold. Cut the cheese in flakes; put it in a small silver or tin dish, made for the purpose, and which may be procured at Adams' Ironmongery showrooms, Haymarket; set the cheese either in the oven or before the fire to toast or melt, and as soon as it becomes thoroughly dissolved, stir it together with a pat of butter, mignionette [ground] pepper and mustard; and let it be eaten instantly with dry toast, or pulled bread."

Cook in a fondue pot; if you don't own one, use a small saucepan from which you can pour the cheese easily.

Incidentally, Mr. Francatelli's Adams' Ironmongery must have been a joyous store to browse in, with the latest in Victorian stewpans, and copper pots with beautiful, firm brass handles, all hanging on display— what a contrast to our modern light ware!

Canapés should be tasty and decorative. They make useful, nutritious "bites" ideal to serve with salad if you want to trim it up.

These cheese canapés could double as savories, the little niblet that puts *finis* to a dignified English dinner, and which you can substitute for a gooey dessert. Little toasted squares of Welsh Rarebit (or Rabbit) can do the same duty.

Cheese Canapés

Francatelli's *Cook's Guide*, 1888

"Cut some slices of stale bread about the twelfth part of an inch in thickness, stamp these out with a plain tin cutter of round, oval, or heart shape, and having fried these croutons in a little clarified butter, of a light colour, dispose some pieces of cheese upon each, with a little mustard spread under the cheese, and seasoned with pepper; push the canapés in a brisk oven or before a clear fire, and as soon as the cheese is melted, serve quite hot.

"*Note*—Toasted cheese served in this fashion is preferable to any other mode, owing to the fact that no time is lost in seasoning and conveying it to the toast."

In place of clarified butter you can use a light oil, such as soybean or walnut. Undoubtedly, Francatelli used white bread which is fairly easy to slice wafer-thin. Wholewheat's another matter; it must be stale, and even so your slices are likely to be thicker than Francatelli's, and you may have trouble cutting the bread with a cookie cutter. If so, keep the job simple by cutting squares and triangles only with your sharpest knife.

Welsh Rarebit

Filippini's *The Table*, 1889

"Take one pound of American cheese; cut up in small pieces. Place them in a sautoire [double-boiler], adding half a [wine] glassful of good ale. Season with half a saltspoonful of red pepper. Stir it continually with a wooden spoon until the mass is well melted, which will take about ten minutes. Have six nice, fresh, large pieces of toast; arrange them on a very hot dish, and distribute the preparation equally over, serving the rarebit very hot."

Natural foods ingredients to serve six:

1 lb American cheese
½ (wine)glass ale; use 1 tbsp or more as needed

pinch of chili powder to taste
6 slices of wholewheat bread, toasted

If you like your rarebit simple, try the following:

Welsh Rarebit au Gratin

Filippini's *The Table*, 1889

"Prepare six toasts of American bread; broil them lightly, remove, and cover each with a slice of Swiss cheese a little less than half an inch thick; lay them in a roasting pan, sprinkling a very little pepper over. Put in the oven for ten minutes. Arrange the toasts on a very hot dish, and send to the table."

These call for baking in that handy little gadget, the toaster oven.

Golden Buck

Top your Welsh Rarebit with a poached egg—and call it Golden Buck.

I've yet to find a human who'll turn down cheese straws—and they're popular too with dogs and some cats. Apparently, Hugo Ziemann and Mrs. Gillette agree, because their recipe for Cheese Straws is zippy and cheesy and irresistible. Serve with salad in place of bread for a summer lunch, and store the leftovers in an airtight tin or jar; reheat, if you wish.

Cayenne Cheese Straws

Hugo Ziemann and Mrs. Gillette's
White House Cook Book, 1887

"A quarter of a pound of flour, 2 oz. butter, 2 oz. grated parmesan cheese, a pinch of salt, and a few grains of cayenne pepper. Mix into a paste with the yolk of an egg. Roll out to the thickness of a silver quarter, about four or five inches long; cut into strips about a third of an inch wide, twist them as you would a paper spill, and lay them on a baking sheet slightly floured. Bake in a moderate oven until crisp, but they must not be the least brown. If put away in a tin, these cheese straws will keep a long time. Serve cold, piled tastefully on a glass dish. You can make the straws of remnants of puff pastry, rolling in the grated cheese."

Try adding a pinch of celery salt—unusual and terrific.

Caution: Use only the *pastry grind* of wholewheat flour.

Natural foods ingredients for about fifty straws:

¼ lb (½ c) wholewheat flour, pastry grind

2 oz (¼ c) butter or margarine

2 oz (¼ c) grated Parmesan cheese

pinch of sea salt

small pinch cayenne

yolk of 1 fertilized egg

You can add:

a pinch or so of celery salt;
a few drops of onion juice.

❧

If tossing omelets is not your forte, then invest in a pan made specially to give you expert sleight of hand, and which consists of two omelet-shaped pans hinged together. Captured inside, your omelet flips over easily as you turn over the double-sided pot.

Cheese Omelet

365 Breakfast Dishes, 1901

"Put 2 tablespoonfuls of butter into a frying pan and when heated add 10 well-beaten eggs and 2 tablespoonfuls of grated Swiss cheese, a pinch of salt and pepper. When done turn out carefully on a hot platter and dust the top with a little grated Parmesan cheese. Put back in the oven for 2 seconds and serve."

Natural foods ingredients to serve four to five:

2 tbsp butter
10 well-beaten eggs, fertilized
2 tbsp grated Swiss cheese

sea salt
pepper
a little grated Parmesan cheese

You can add:

a half-pinch of cayenne;
a little whey.

And for lovers of fondue, here's one that may have been whipped up for a presidential snack back in the 1880s.

This "fondue" is a hybrid—halfway between fondue and soufflé.

For a quick and easy dip-in fondue, see my Fake Fondue (*200 Really Great Natural Foods Recipes*; Ballantine, 1972), which also neglects the real fondue cheese, Swiss Gruyère, in favor of cheddar or home-grown Swiss from the nation's dairy state, Wisconsin.

Cheese Fondue

Hugo Ziemann and Mrs. Gillette's
White House Cook Book, 1887

"Melt an ounce of butter, and whisk into it a pint of boiled milk. Dissolve two tablespoonfuls of flour in a gill of cold milk, add it to the boiled milk and let it cool. Beat the yolks of four eggs with a heaping teaspoonful of salt, half a teaspoonful of pepper, and five ounces of grated cheese. Whip the whites of the eggs and add them, pour the mixture into a deep tin lined (around the sides) with buttered paper, and allow for the rising, say four inches. Bake twenty minutes and serve the moment it leaves the oven."

Natural foods ingredients to serve four:

1 oz (1 tbsp) butter or margarine
1 pt (2 c) boiled milk *plus* ¼ c cold
2 tbsp wholewheat flour

4 fertilized eggs
1½ tsp sea salt
pinch pepper
5 oz grated cheddar-type cheese

❧

Cheese Soufflé

Hugo Ziemann and Mrs. Gillette's
White House Cook Book, 1887

"Melt an ounce of butter in a saucepan; mix
smoothly with it one ounce of flour, a pinch of salt
and cayenne and a quarter of a pint of milk; simmer
the mixture gently over the fire, stirring all the time,
till it is as thick as melted butter; stir into it about
three ounces of finely grated parmesan, or any good
cheese. Turn it into a basin, and mix with it the
yolks of two well-beaten eggs. Whisk three whites to
a solid froth, and just before the soufflé is baked put
them into it, and pour the mixture into a small round
tin. It should be only half filled, as the fondu will
rise very high. Pin a napkin around the dish in which
it is baked, and serve the moment it is baked. It
would be well to have a metal cover strongly heated.
Time twenty minutes. Sufficient for six persons."

First, check Mrs. Beeton's TO MAKE A SOUFFLÉ.
This is a very delicate, high-rising soufflé—Mrs.
Gillette uses extra egg whites—so her point about the
metal cover is well taken; any jolt, sudden draft, or
wobbling at the knees, and the delicate beauty can
lurch into a catastrophe of cheese and eggs. So use a
heated lid to ward off drafts—and hobgoblins.
Note the extra egg white for added lift.

Natural foods ingredients to serve four:

1 oz (1 tbsp) butter or
   margarine
1 oz (1 tbsp) whole-
   grain flour, pastry
   grind
pinch sea salt
pinch cayenne

¼ pt (½ c) fresh milk
3 oz Parmesan cheese,
   finely grated
yolks of 2 fertilized eggs,
   well-beaten
whites of 3 fertilized eggs

You can add:

whey in place of milk.

∾

Eggs Baked with Cheese

365 Breakfast Dishes, 1901

"In a flat earthen dish [or casserole], melt 1 teaspoonful of butter and let it run over the bottom of
the dish. Cover with thin slices of cheese and dust
with white pepper and a little salt. Break in carefully as many eggs as the dish will hold and place in
a hot oven until the whites are set; then serve at
once."

Choose a good cooking cheese, such as Swiss or one
of the Monterey Jack–type goat cheeses.

Natural foods ingredients:

1 tsp butter or oil
slices of cheese
white pepper

a little sea salt
fertilized eggs

∾

Although the fourth earl of Sandwich gave his name to America's most popular luncheon dish, the idea of eating food spread on bread dates back to the days of Christ as part of the Jewish Passover ceremonies, when unleavened bread is eaten with chopped nuts and apple, and bitter herbs. The Earl of Sandwich's inspiration notwithstanding, oldtime housewives mostly ignored this easy-to-fix dish until the latter part of the nineteenth century, when a few recipes appear featuring chopped meat put between bread. But this was distinctly convenience food—probably the first on record.

Francatelli for instance packed Prince Albert's lunchbox, taken on shooting expeditions in the cold wilds of Scotland, with sandwiches made of his favorite game, partridge. He also gives a recipe for sandwiches to be served at a ball-supper—hardly school-lunch foodstuff. On the other hand, Mrs. Rundell suggests spreading Orange Butter between sweet cookies, a great idea for a quick and unusual dessert (see ORANGE BUTTER).

How did people manage without sandwiches? Easily. Good housewives like Eliza Smith baked enormous, savory "pyes," a juicy chunk making an easily handled light lunch; while a whole pie and a batch of Johnny (Journey) cakes could sustain a traveler over many miles.

Cheese Sandwiches

Hugo Ziemann and Mrs. Gillette's
White House Cook Book, 1887

"These are extremely nice, and are very easily made. Take one hard-boiled egg, a quarter of a pound of common cheese grated, half a teaspoonful of salt, half a teaspoonful of pepper, half a teaspoonful of mustard, one tablespoonful of melted butter, and one tablespoonful of . . . cold water. Take the yolk of the egg and put it into a small bowl and crumble it down, put into it the butter and mix it smooth with a spoon, then add the salt, pepper, mustard, and the cheese, mixing each well. Then put in the tablespoonful of vinegar, which will make it the proper thickness. If vinegar is not relished, then use cold water instead. Spread this between two biscuits or pieces of oat-cake, and you could not require a better sandwich. Some people will prefer the sandwiches less highly seasoned. In that case, season to taste."

Mrs. Gillette's idea of using oatcakes lifts this sandwich out of the mundane; you can use other wholegrain breads, too.

A *useful tip:* Keep hardboiled eggs on hand for last-minute sandwiches and garnishes (on curries, vegetables, etc.).

Natural foods ingredients for one hefty sandwich:

1 fertilized egg, hard-boiled	pinch of dried mustard *or* ½ tsp prepared
4 oz cheddar style cheese, grated	1 tbsp melted butter
½ tsp of sea salt	1 tbsp cold water
½ tsp pepper (or less)	1 tbsp vinegar
	2 wholegrain oatcakes

You can add:

any wholegrain bread in place of oatcakes.

❧

Some Dishes with Beans and Rice

ODDLY, few recipes for beans appear in oldtime cookbooks, probably because their readers consumed so much meat. And of course, the soybean, that protein staple of the Orient, was unknown in this country until a few decades ago.

Beans are a highly concentrated food, having carbohydrates and incomplete protein, and should be eaten sparingly. Soybeans are the exception; they contain complete protein, no carbohydrates, and make an excellent substitute for meat.

In 1872, Dr. Dio Lewis published *Our Digestion; or, My Jolly Friend's Secret,* a book full of amusing anecdotes and crackling good advice. Dr. Lewis rails convincingly agin chewing or smoking tobacco, overweight, and of course indigestion, which he considers the cause of most bodily evils.

Here is his recipe for Bean Porridge. Serve it with a heaping pile of alkali-forming carrots and green vegetables; both meat and beans are acid.

Bean Porridge

Dr. Dio Lewis's *Our Digestion,* 1872

"Every one knows how to make bean porridge (baked beans), though perhaps it may be well to state that the salt should not be introduced until the porridge is nearly done.

"Some cooks have the fancy that no other meat than pork will do to boil with the beans, but beef is quite as good, and chicken is still better than either beef or pork. We have all learned that bean porridge improves with age, for who has not heard the lines:

'Bean porridge hot, bean porridge cold
Bean porridge best when it's nine days old.' "

Cook your beans as the doctor dictates (preferably in an old-fashioned American beanpot), for from four to six hours. Beans previously soaked take less cooking time.

Note: Contrary to the advice given in most oldtime cook books (and some modern ones) soaking water should not be thrown away (it contains vitamins leached from the vegetable or legume) but used, the amount being added according to that given in the recipe.

Mrs. Henderson got this lima bean recipe from a London cooking-teacher who, to judge by the following, turned out rattling good cooks:

Lima Beans

Mrs. Henderson's *Practical Cooking*, 1876

"Put a pint of shelled beans into boiling water slightly salted, adding two or three slices of onion. When tender, drain them. Put butter the size of an egg into a heated saucepan, and when it is hot add an even tablespoonful of minced onions, [and] cook well. Then put in the beans; add enough water (or better, stock) to keep them moist. Keep them at the side of the fire about a quarter of an hour, as it takes them some time to soak; just before taking them out, add a small handful of minced parsley. Do not cook them much after adding the parsley, as that spoils its color."

Reserve the water drained from the beans, add a little yeast extract, and use as the stock Mrs. Henderson recommends.

Mrs. Henderson, of course, does not realize that as her parsley's deep color fades away, so do its vitamins.

Natural foods ingredients to serve six to eight:

1 pt (2 c) shelled lima beans	1 tbsp minced onions
sea salt	minced parsley
2 or 3 slices onion	pepper to taste
butter the size of an egg (2 tbsp)	

You can add:

yeast extract to the drained vegetable water for stock.

❧

I am sorry to say that the rice used during the nineteenth century was white, not natural brown; by this time denatured cereals had acquired their high, but devitalized, social standing, nutritious wholegrain being usually regarded as peasant food.

From the laboratory comes proof of the enormous difference in nutritional value between white and brown rice. One cup white rice (191 grams) contains 24 mg. of calcium, as opposed to 39 mg. in a cup of regular commercial brown rice; 136 mg. of phosphorus as opposed to 303 in brown rice; 0.8 mg. iron as opposed to 2.0 mg.; 0.07 mg. of B_1, as opposed to 0.32 in brown rice.*

---

* *Nutritional Data*, H. J. Heinz Co., third edition, 1956

Adjustments must be made on account of the bulk of white rice, which sits lighter in a cup (191 grams) than brown rice, which weighs in at 208 grams per cup.

You can also figure that *natural* brown rice is more nutritious still; only its inedible outer husk is removed.

Yet, even with variables, these figures give an idea of the extent of nutritional loss that results from denaturing; no wonder manufacturers stress the enrichment of their nonwholegrain products; without it, white rice is a sorry food indeed—and still deficient with it.

Despite Thomas Jefferson's enthusiastic research into the subject—he virtually started the rice industry in this country, making a practical hobby of collecting new strains on his travels abroad, and coercing his friends to do the same—rice apparently was not considered an important food until toward the end of the nineteenth century. Here and there in the earlier cookbooks, you'll find a few rice recipes tucked into the dessert and bread sections, rice cake and rice pudding being the most popular.

Regarded at this time as a vegetable, yet included as a cereal-ingredient in bread and cakes, rice in America had to await the arrival of the great turn-of-the-century chefs and the modern natural-foods cooks to be appreciated as a principal food in the manner of the East.

Perhaps this is why Lafcadio Hearn gives few rice dishes in his otherwise fascinating *La Cuisine Créole;* the recipe for Jambalaya below is the one and only of this truly Southern rice dish in his book. I hope he's put to shame in his celestial kitchen for not giving us at least a choice.

Jambalaya of Fowls and Rice

Lafcadio Hearn's *La Cuisine Créole*,
1885

"Cut up and stew a fowl; when half done, add a cup of rice, a slice of ham minced, and pepper and salt; let all cook together until the rice swells and absorbs all the gravy of the stewed chicken, but it must not be allowed to get hard or dry. Serve in a deep dish. Southern children are very fond of this; it is said to be an Indian dish, and very wholesome as well as palatable; it can be made of many things."

❧

On the other hand, the little band of elegant house-wife-chefs (who included, incidentally, the famous Mrs. Lincoln, author of *The Boston Cookbook* published in 1887) found rice a useful breakfast cereal.

And anyway, it tastes good any time—day, evening, or night.

Eggs on Rice

365 Breakfast Dishes, 1901

"Butter a baking dish, fill it half full with well seasoned boiled rice; make as many depressions in the rice as there are people to be served; break an egg into each of these, sprinkle with salt and strew with bits of butter. Bake until the eggs are set. Serve hot."

Natural foods ingredients to serve four:

4 c cooked natural brown   sea salt
  rice   bits of butter or margarine
4 fertilized eggs   (about 1 tbsp)

❧

Rice Omelet

365 Breakfast Dishes, 1901

"To 1 cup of cold boiled rice add 1 cup of milk, 3 well beaten eggs, salt, pepper and a teaspoonful of butter. Pour into a hot well greased omelet pan. Cook until a light brown. Garnish with parsley."

Natural foods ingredients to make one large individual omelet:

1 c cold, boiled natural
   brown rice
1 c milk
3 fertilized eggs, well-
   beaten
sea salt

pepper
1 tsp butter
oil for frying
sprigs of parsley for
   garnish

This is Mrs. D. A. Lincoln's contribution:

Turkish Croquettes

365 Breakfast Dishes, 1901

"Stew ½ a can of tomatoes fifteen minutes with one slice each of onion, carrot and turnip, one teaspoonful of herbs, one sprig of parsley, two cloves, two peppercorns, one teaspoonful salt and one saltspoonful of pepper. Rub through a strainer. Take one cup of the strained tomatoes, one cup of brown soup stock, season highly and when boiling add one scant cup of uncooked rice. Cook until the liquor is absorbed. Add a quarter of a cup of butter and cook on the back of the stove [simmer] until the rice is soft. Add one beaten egg and a little cream sauce or thick tomato sauce, using enough to make it quite moist. When cool, shape into rolls. Roll in fine bread crumbs, then in egg, then in crumbs again, and fry in smoking hot fat. Sometimes it is better to parboil the rice for five minutes, as it is more difficult to soften it in the stock than in clear water."

Parboil natural brown rice for half an hour, using 1½ cups water to 1 cup rice. For protein, add a little soy flour.

For hints on making croquettes, see CROQUETTES.

Natural foods ingredients to serve four:

1 small can tomatoes
1 slice each: onion, carrot, turnip
1 tsp mixed herbs
1 sprig parsley
2 cloves
2 peppercorns
1 tsp sea salt
1½ c water
pinch of pepper
1 c stock

1 scant c natural brown rice
¼ c butter
1 fertilized egg, beaten, *plus* 1 more for dipping
a little CREAM SAUCE *or* TOMATO SAUCE
breadcrumbs
oil for frying

❧

﹏❦ 5 ❦﹏

Vegetables and Salads—
God's Gift to the Universe

To make a Cabbage-Lettuce Pye.

TAKE some of the largest and hardest Cabbage-Lettuce you can get; boil them in Salt and Water till they are tender; then lay them in a Colander to drain dry; then have your Paste laid in your Pattipan ready, and lay Butter on the bottom; then lay in your Lettuce and some Artichoke-bottoms, and some large pieces of Marrow, and the yolks of eight hard Eggs, and some scalded Sorrel; bake it, and when it comes out of the Oven, cut open the Lid, and pour in a Caudle made with White-wine and Sugar, and thickened with Eggs; so serve it hot.

Eliza Smith's *The Compleat Housewife*, 1727

Vegetable Dishes—Plain and Fancy

It's hard to believe that Eliza Smith baked this imaginative Cabbage-Lettuce Pye either as a side dish or, more likely, for a fasting day. Its enticing combination of lettuce, sorrel, cabbage, artichoke bottoms, and marrow (kohlrabi), highlighted with hardboiled eggs and sweetened with white wine, deserves center stage.

If you plan to adapt this recipe, I suggest you parbake the pastry cases first, using a short pastry. Cook the vegetables lightly, then combine. Dot with butter and continue baking for only ten minutes or enough time to melt the butter and let it sink in—thus helping conserve the minerals and vitamins of which Eliza Smith knew nothing, only that overcooked food was not so tasty.

Then with a sharp knife carefully cut a triangular slice out of the edge of the top crust; pour the sauce through this hole, and replace the piece of piecrust. If it won't adhere, stick with the cook's equivalent of Elmer's—white of egg.

Toward the end of the nineteenth century, Dr. Lewis's *Our Digestion, or My Jolly Friend's Secret* led the trickle of books on health that has turned into today's still flowing torrent. Cooks began to learn about minerals and vitamins, although few took the lessons to heart, still cooking vegetables to a tasteless pulp which they enlivened by adding condiments, and soda for retaining color.

When cooking the vegetable dishes that follow, therefore, use your favorite nutrition-conserving method of steaming, searing, or cooking waterless. For

instance, in Asparagus with Eggs, searing the vegetables in a wok may be enough preliminary cooking.

Asparagus with Eggs

Hugo Ziemann and Mrs. Gillette's
White House Cook Book, 1887

"Boil a bunch of asparagus twenty minutes; cut off
the tender tops and lay them in a deep pie plate,
buttering, salting and peppering well. Beat up four
eggs, the yolks and whites separately, to a stiff froth;
(pour together into a bowl,) add two tablespoonfuls of milk or cream, a tablespoonful of warm
butter, pepper and salt to taste. Pour evenly over the
asparagus mixture. Bake eight minutes or until the
eggs are set. Very good."

Agreed, especially if you bring out the flavor of the
asparagus by steaming or searing a minimal time.

Natural foods ingredients to serve four:

1 bunch of asparagus   pepper
  (about 1½ lb)   4 fertilized eggs
a little butter *plus* 1 tbsp   2 tbsp fresh milk or
sea salt   cream

You can add:

broccoli in place of asparagus.

❧

Corn was a popular vegetable with oldtime cooks, who usually served it dressed up with other ingredients. They were wiser than they knew: corn is the least nutritious of all grains, contains incomplete protein, and is poor in vitamins. On the plus side, both white and yellow corn are rich in potassium, phosphorus, and sulphur acids.

So if you're nutrition-conscious, don't serve corn too often, even though Mrs. Gillette and Mr. Ziemann may feel hurt—their recipe's delicious.

Corn Pudding

Hugo Ziemann and Mrs. Gillette's
White House Cook Book, 1887

"This is a Virginia dish. Scrape the substance out of twelve ears of tender, green, uncooked corn (it is better scraped than grated, as you do not get those husky particles which you cannot avoid with a grater); add yolks and whites, beaten separately, of four eggs, a teaspoonful of sugar, the same of flour mixed in a tablespoonful of butter, a small quantity of salt and pepper and one pint of milk. Bake about half or three quarters of an hour."

Natural foods ingredients:

12 ears of corn, ripe   sea salt
 4 fertilized eggs   pepper
 1 tsp sugar   1 pt (2 c) milk
 1 tsp wholewheat flour
 1 tbsp butter or
   margarine

You can add:

honey in place of sugar.

∾

Eggplant Stuffed with Nuts

Marion Harland and Christine
Herrick's *Modern Cooking*, 1904

"Boil the whole plant until tender, scoop out;
chop fine 1 cupful hickory or other nuts; add 1 tablespoonful butter, season with salt and pepper; add 1
tablespoonful bread crumbs and 2 eggs well beaten.
Fill shell with mixture, and bake one hour."

Good eating—particularly if you toast the nuts and
breadcrumbs before stuffing.

Natural foods ingredients to serve four:

1 medium sized eggplant
1 c nut meats, chopped
1 tbsp butter, margarine,
　or oil
sea salt to taste

pepper
1 tbsp wholewheat bread-
　crumbs
2 fertilized eggs, beaten

❧

Mushrooms hold at least one macabre distinction. Agrippa did in his old enemy, Claudius, by getting him to eat a succulent plateful of a good and deadly kind. One can understand Claudius digging in without noting first if his taster dropped dead—a fatal oversight in those ruthless days.

But, as Pliny remarked, mushrooms are "the food of the Gods," so at least Claudius departed for Mount Olympus stuffed appropriately and delectably.

Mushrooms (of the *non*deadly variety) make an unusual, if overly light, breakfast—they contain a smidgen of protein and not much else.

So if you're a busy person who likes to kick off the day with a good breakfast, pile up extra slices of wholegrain toast spread with nut butter.

Mushrooms on Toast

365 Breakfast Dishes, 1901

"Put 2 cups of mushrooms in a stew pan with 2 tablespoonfuls of butter rolled in a little flour; add 1 teaspoonful of salt, a pinch of cayenne and a squeeze of lemon juice; stew gently until the mushrooms are tender. Serve on toast."

Natural foods ingredients to serve four:

2 c mushrooms, chopped, sliced, or whole	1 tsp sea salt
2 tbsp butter or margarine	pinch of cayenne
a little wholewheat flour	a little lemon juice
	4 slices wholegrain toast

Peas and potatoes for breakfast? Why not—potatoes provide good energy food, while peas are one of the richest sources of vegetable protein. However, the vitamin C of the latter escapes with shelling, so resist getting a head start by doing this job the night before.

Many oldtime cooks worked in kitchens overlooking the kitchen garden; their time taken from picking to serving peas could be as little as thirty minutes. Few of us are so lucky.

Peas in Potato Cases

365 Breakfast Dishes, 1901

"Mash 6 or 8 boiled potatoes. Add butter and milk in the usual way. When well mashed add a little flour to slightly stiffen them. Fill greased patty pans with the potatoes, putting a piece of bread in the center of each. When they are browned turn them out carefully; take out the bread and in the hollow made by it, fill with young . . . cooked peas, which have been seasoned with a little cream, pepper and salt. Serve on a hot platter."

Natural foods ingredients to serve six:

6 or 8 boiled potatoes	1½ c cooked peas
butter (1 tbsp)	a little cream
a little milk	sea salt
a little wholewheat flour	pepper
6 to 8 slices of bread	

You can add:

yogurt in place of cream.

See *200 Really Great Natural Foods Recipes,* page 147: "Extra-Good Mashed Potatoes."

☙

You can make this pepper recipe fully nutritious by adding a little soy flour or sunflower meal to the sauce.

Stuffed Peppers

Table Talk, 1901

"Take 3 green peppers, wash them, then put them in hot grease and blanch until tender. Remove from the fire and again wipe the skin with a cloth. Cut off the tops and take out the seeds. Take 1 oz. of butter, chop up a few shallots and fry in the butter, adding a few chopped mushrooms. Season with tomato puree, thickened with bread crumbs, and put this filling into the peppers. Place on the dish and serve with [white] sauce."

In the first step, the peppers are actually deep-fat fried; so put into a wire basket and dunk until tender.

Natural foods ingredients to serve three:

3 large green peppers
oil for frying
1 oz butter
a few shallots
a few (½ c) chopped
  mushrooms

(1 tbsp) tomato puree
(⅓ c) breadcrumbs,
  wholegrain
1 c ECONOMICAL WHITE
  SAUCE

You can add:

TOMATO SAUCE in place of ECONOMICAL WHITE SAUCE; soy flour or sunflower meal to the sauce.

❧

The simplest, and most delicious, dish is surely a gigantic baked potato topped with butter along the opening cut into its light brown jacket. Although nearly three-quarters water when cooked, potatoes are good energy food, and for a vegetable, high in protein —which can be added to if you replace butter with nut or soybean spread.

If your conscience pricks you as you reach for the calorie-full butter, remember that potatoes contain next to no fat. So dig in and enjoy. As we noted, before, the forebears of those good-looking Irish-Americans were reared in the Old Country mainly on potatoes.

In the New Country, potatoes were known to New Englanders during the seventeenth century and were dished up at Harvard in 1708, as an old menu card proves. Actually, the vegetable originated in Peru and was brought to Europe by the Spaniards; it returned to this side of the Atlantic in one of those food migrations that are so fascinating—this time courtesy the British.

By the time Miss Shute wrote her cook book, the potato was well-established on American soil, despite the hazard of a blight that swept the crops here and in Europe (of which more anon).

Baked Potatoes

Miss Shute's *American Housewife,* 1879

"Wash and wipe them; put them into the oven with the skins on, and bake from three quarters of an hour to an hour. When almost half done, prick them all over with a fork; or if that is not done, break them a little as soon as you find they are done; this is to let out the steam and prevent them from getting soggy."

Broiled Potatoes

Miss Shute's *American Housewife,*
1879

"Parboil, then slice and broil them til they are
nicely browned. To be eaten with butter and salt."

Here are some more hints:

Hints on Cooking Potatoes

Always cook potatoes with their skins on; first
scrub, then remove the nobby bits. This way their
flavor is really delicious because there's no vitamin
loss through peeling, while the skin itself tastes good.

Add a pinch of nutmeg to mashed or cream potatoes.

Vary Miss Shute's recipe by brushing oil or melted
butter over baked potatoes before cooking.

Add chips of American cheese, or grated cheese
such as Swiss, to mashed potatoes as you prepare
them.

Use leftover potato water in muffins and breads in
place of milk.

✎

This is the real, old-fashioned way of making potato pancakes, i.e., using raw instead of cooked potato. Use the recipe as a base for other flavors, such as herb, carrot, cheese, etc.

Potato Pancake

Mrs. Gesine Lemcke in *365 Breakfast Dishes*, 1901

"Wash and grate 12 large raw potatoes. [Dry well.] Mix with 1 tablespoonful of salt and the yolks of 3 eggs. Beat the whites to a stiff froth; add the potatoes slowly to the whites. Place a large frying pan with 1 tablespoonful of fat over the fire as soon as hot. Put small portions from the mixture with a spoon into the hot fat to form cakes the size of a saucer; bake light brown on both sides. Serve on a big plate."

Natural foods ingredients to serve twelve:

12 large raw potatoes   3 fertilized eggs
  1 tbsp sea salt   oil for frying

You can add:

pinch of thyme, or other herb;
a little grated carrot;
cheese or nuts;
a sweet sauce and serve as dessert.

Although sweet potatoes are not a regular potato—they're actually a root belonging to the morning-glory family—they, too, are a good food with iron and plenty of the B vitamins, and vitamin C.

Sweet Potato Roulettes and Bacon

365 Breakfast Dishes, 1901

"Boil and mash the sweet potatoes; add a little salt and pepper and 1 tablespoonful of butter to each [2 cups of potatoes], mixing while hot. Mould into small round balls and fry in deep hot fat. Drain for a moment on [a paper towel]. Then pile them neatly on a dish, and serve bacon cooked crisp around them."

Add a little honey for the sweet tooth in the family.

Natural foods ingredients to serve four:

4 sweet potatoes	oil for frying
sea salt	slices of bacon
pepper	
1 tbsp butter or margarine	

You can add:

sesame seeds, roasted and sprinkled over, in place of bacon;
1 tbsp chestnut flour to the mixture, with a little milk for moisture.

Other ideas:

When serving sweet potatoes mashed, top with grated coconut.

An old Southern belle gave me this recipe:

Brush the insides of orange halves (skins only) with butter; fill with the above potato mixture and bake for twenty minutes. Delicious.

Make mashed sweet potatoes using two-thirds the regular quantity, and one-third mashed banana. Sprinkle grated nutmeg over it before serving.

❧

Here's a "beginner's luck" recipe—meaning you can't fail, especially if you use fresh and not leftover vegetables. The latter lose vitamins and minerals in the second cooking—and their rich, healthy flavor, too, of course.

Toss in a few chopped walnuts or almonds; or garnish with hard-boiled eggs, allowing one per person.

Vegetable Curry

Table Talk, 1901

"Pour ½ a pt. of boiling water mixed with 1 tablespoonful of curry powder into 2 tablespoonfuls butter in which a large onion has been fried and add salt and lemon juice. After cooking this for five minutes, add 1 pt. of green peas, 1 turnip, 3 carrots and 3 potatoes, all having been cooked previously. Let them remain in the curry for 10 minutes, and serve all together."

Parboil the turnip, carrots and potatoes. Let them finish cooking in the curry sauce.

Natural foods ingredients to serve four:

½ pt (1 c) boiling water
1 tbsp CURRY POWDER
2 tbsp butter or
   margarine
1 large onion
sea salt

juice of ½ lemon
1 pt (2 c) peas
1 turnip, parboiled
3 carrots, parboiled
3 small potatoes,
   parboiled

You can add:

hard-boiled eggs, sliced, 1 per person;
½ cup chopped nuts, such as almonds or walnuts.

❧

Salads—Some from an English Garden

Poet's Recipe for Salad

The Reverend Sydney Smith, quoted
in *Modern Cooking*, 1904

"Two boiled potatoes, passed through kitchen sieve,
Softness and smoothness to the salad give;
Of Mordant mustard add a single spoon,
Distrust the condiment that bites too soon;
Yet deem it not, thou man of taste, a fault
To add a double quantity of salt;
Four times the spoon with oil of Lucca crown,
And twice with vinegar procured from town;
The flavor needs it, and your poet begs
The pounded yellow of two well-boiled eggs;
Let onions' atoms lurk within the bowl,
And scarce suspected, animate the whole;
And, lastly, in the flavored compound toss
A magic teaspoon of anchovy sauce,
Oh, great and glorious! Oh, herbaceous meat!
'Twould tempt the dying anchoret to eat;
Back to the world he'd turn his weary soul
And dip his finger in the salad bowl.
Then, though green turtle fail, though venison's
        tough,
And ham and turkey are not boiled enough,
Serenely full, the epicure may say:
'Fate cannot harm me—I have dined today' "

Reverend Sydney Smith's delightful commentary on salads was often quoted in oldtime cookbooks. The poet-priest lived in an age of oratory, when lawyers made flowery speeches in court and young ladies studied elocution. But the sentiment, though often gooey by our tougher standards, was genuinely romantic. It was an age too that loved botany and food, and it is all brought together by the charming reverend in his poem.

But now to the practical side of cooking, and wisdom from Miss Shute on the washing of vegetables:

Effect of Washing upon Vegetables

Miss Shute's *American Housewife*, 1879

"The peculiar flavor of all kinds of vegetables is affected by washing; but of all kinds, that used for salads is especially impaired by water. These should, therefore, never be washed unless necessary, and then only immediately before preparation for the table, and as rapidly as possible, all the water being removed by whirling or shaking in a colander."

Sprayed vegetables, bought from a store, must of course be well washed. However, unsprayed vegetables grown in your own garden should be treated as Miss Shute suggests.

For would-be vegetable growers without a garden, the U.S. Department of Agriculture has come out with a leaflet written specially for you, entitled *Minigardens for Vegetables*. The writer tells you how to grow lettuce, carrots, cucumbers, etc., in window-boxes, old pails, and even plastic bags. You can get this little pamphlet from the Superintendent of Documents, U.S. Government Printing Office, Washington, D.C. 30402, at the incredible price of fifteen cents.

Celery Salad

Filippini's *The Table*, 1889

"If the heads of celery be large and white, use two; if they should be small, use three. Pare off the green stalks, trim the roots nice, and cut it into short shreds; wash thoroughly in cold water, lift it up with the hands and drain in a cloth. When well drained, place the celery in a salad-bowl, and season with a pinch of salt, half a pinch of pepper, and one and a half wooden salad-spoonfuls of vinegar, also the same quantity of oil. Mix well, and serve."

Wash the celery *before* shredding to conserve vitamins. Garnish with sprigs of inner leaves, saving the dark, outer ones for cooking with a mixture of potatoes, carrots, and parsley.

In *The Table*, Filippini gives three versions of Dandelion Salad: plain, with hard-boiled eggs quartered and laid over the dandelion leaves (very pretty), and lastly combined with cooked beetroot cut into thin slices. All are dressed simply with seasoning, oil, and vinegar.

On the other hand, Francatelli gives few salads in his book, published only a year before Filippini's, which is significant. Filippini was king in the famous Delmonico's kitchen; Francatelli lorded it over Queen Victoria's table, where the salad had not yet become fashionable. Nevertheless, Francatelli's Dandelion Salad is redolent of the lush English countryside, and here it is. Notice he suggests using lemon juice in place of vinegar.

Dandelion Salad

Francatelli's Cook's Guide, 1888

"The tender green leaves of young field dandelions are used for salad. To prepare for serving, wash several times in cold water, drain well, put into a dish and cut fine. . . . Mix six tablespoonfuls of oil with three of vinegar or lemon juice and a quarter teaspoonful of pepper. Pour over the leaves, toss well and serve."

These field dandelion leaves (obtainable from a good health foods store) make a delicious and delicate salad, with its own sweet-sour flavor.

Don't substitute those dandelion leaves peeking up in the lawn—they're tough, and bitter-tasting.

❧

All Mr. Francatelli's salads sound so beautiful; I can picture this handsome, elderly gentleman, pottering about his garden after a fine English rain, gathering the rich, dark leaves for this beautiful salad.

English Salad

Francatelli's Cook's Guide, 1888

"Rinse and immediately wipe with a soft cloth the leaves of a ripe cos lettuce; split down the stalk, and divide each half leaf into four pieces; place these in a salad bowl with a few fresh-gathered leaves of green mint; season with one tablespoonful of salad-oil, two of vinegar, a dessert-spoonful of moist sugar, pepper and salt; mix and serve."

For "ripe cos lettuce" read "romaine lettuce with rich dark green leaves."

Another English Salad

Francatelli's *Cook's Guide*, 1888

"Take equal parts of lettuce; shred celery, watercress, small salad [herbs], beetroot [leaves], and spring radishes; thoroughly wash them for a few minutes, and when drained in a cloth, gather up the four corners into the right hand, and shake out all the water. Next put the salad in a bowl; season with equal proportion of oil and vinegar, two or three chopped green onions, pepper and salt. Mix and serve."

I find this old-style method of drying salad the easiest and best; the greens, of course, should be thoroughly dry before you add the dressing.

Mr. Francatelli omits one important step: soaking leafy vegetables in salt water to draw out and destroy bugs lurking in those fresh, green leaves straight from the garden.

Natural foods ingredients:

Equal parts of:

lettuce
celery
watercress
pinch of *fines herbes or*
   your choice of herbs
beetroot leaves
3 or 4 red radishes

salad oil
vinegar
2 or 3 scallions, with
   leaves
pepper
sea salt

You can add:

lemon juice in place of vinegar;
honey to the dressing.

Here are two recipes for lettuce salad—served on its own for once.

Lettuce Lemon Salad

Marion Harland and Christine
Herrick's *Modern Cooking*, 1904

"Arrange a dish of crisp lettuce leaves, with a generous portion of dressing made by stirring together equal quantities lemon juice, sugar, and water until the sugar is dissolved."

In place of sugar, use honey.

Mint Lemon Salad

Marion Harland and Christine
Herrick's *Modern Cooking*, 1904

"This is made the same as lettuce lemon salad, with a few leaves of shredded fresh mint scattered among the lettuce leaves, or put into the dressing five or ten minutes before serving. Lemon points, or slices of lemon, may be used for garnishing any of the salads."

Serve with wholewheat toast, and the following dressing for a nourishing light meal:

Lettuce Salad with Egg Dressing

Marion Harland and Christine
Herrick's *Modern Cooking*, 1904

"Rub the yolks of 3 hard-boiled eggs through a colander; salt to taste, and make a paste by adding 1 dessertspoonful of olive oil; mix thoroughly and dilute by adding gradually ½ teaspoonful lemon juice and ½ teacupful [⅓ cup] water. Pour over the lettuce. This amount of dressing is sufficient for a large sized dish of salad."

Keep life simple—put everything into the blender.

Need a good recipe for leftover champagne and truffles? If so, Filippini has it. Of course, you may be substituting mushrooms and opening a new bottle of domestic best. Don't worry: what the guests don't see, they won't ask for.

Just call your version "The Mikado" and dedicate it to Gilbert and Sullivan.

Japanese Salad

Filippini's *The Table*, 1889

"Mince three medium-sized truffles very fine, also two large, cold, boiled potatoes; put the whole into a bowl, and season with half a pinch each of salt and pepper, and the third of a pinch of nutmeg; pour half a glassful of champagne over all, and let rest for two hours, then add eighteen whole cooked mussels, a teaspoonful of chopped chives, and the same quantity of chopped parsley. Mix all well together, then dress the salad into a bowl, decorating it with six small, white [Bibb] lettuce-leaves and six fillets of anchovies; then serve."

Undoubtedly a gentle giant, Filippini's pinch, so he tells us frequently in *The Table*, measures one whole tablespoonful. What a mitt.

Natural foods ingredients to serve four to six:

- 3 medium-sized truffles or ½ lb mushrooms, washed raw, or cooked
- 2 large boiled potatoes, cold
- 1½ tsp salt
- 1½ tsp pepper
- 1 tsp ground nutmeg
- ½ champagne glass (½ c) champagne
- 18 whole cooked mussels
- 1 tsp chopped chives
- 1 tsp chopped parsley
- 6 leaves from Bibb lettuce
- 6 fillets of anchovies

Who doesn't love potato salad? Here's Miss Shute's recipe, which I'm sure she dished up at countless church picnics—it has that ambiance of good eating, good fellowship, and happy times. Like all good potato salad.

Potato Salad and Salad Dressing

Miss Shute's *American Housewife*,
1879

"Cut a dozen cold boiled potatoes into fancy shapes, one quarter of an inch thick; mix with some flakes of cold boiled fish, halibut, cod or salmon, and pour over them a boiled salad dressing made with six tablespoonfuls of melted butter or salad oil, six tablespoonfuls of cream or milk, one teaspoonful of salt, half a teaspoonful of pepper, and one teaspoonful of ground [dry] mustard. Into this put one [half cup] of vinegar. Boil well; then add three raw eggs beaten to a foam; remove directly from the fire and stir for five minutes. When thoroughly cold turn it over the salad, garnish with slices of pickled cucumbers, beetroot, hard boiled eggs and fresh parsley. The boiled salad [dressing] can be made in quantities and kept tightly bottled for weeks. When used for green salad it should be placed at the bottom of the bowl and the salad on top [ready for mixing at the table] for if mixed (some time before serving) the vegetables lose that crispness which is so delicious to the epicure. Slices of egg [cooked], beet, or cold potatoes serve to ornament the dish."

To cut potatoes into fancy shapes: for tiny balls dig into whole cooked potato with a melon scoop; for triangles and squares cut cooked potato into slices ¼ inch thick, then trim into shape.

Natural foods ingredients for two big bowlfuls:

Potato Salad

12 large boiled potatoes, cold

some (2 lb) boiled fish (any kind)

8 slices pickled cucumbers

8 slices or more cooked beetroot

6 hard-boiled eggs

sprigs of parsley for garnish

Salad Dressing

6 tbsp salad oil (peanut, soy bean, or light sesame)

6 tbsp fresh milk

1 tsp sea salt

pinch of pepper

1 tsp dry mustard

1 c vinegar

3 fertilized eggs, raw

You can add:

canned fish, such as salmon or sardines, in place of boiled fresh;

1 cup raw, grated beet in place of cooked;

lemon in place of vinegar in the dressing;

reconstituted dried milk in place of fresh.

❧

6

Oldfashioned Pies, Puddings, and Other Sweet Goodies

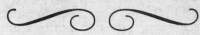

To make a Carrot Pudding.

TAKE raw Carrots, and scrape them clean, grate them with a grater without a back. To half a pound of Carrot, take a pound of grated Bread, a Nutmeg, a little Cinnamon, a very little Salt, half a pound of Sugar, and half a pint of Sack, eight Eggs, a pound of Butter melted, and as much Cream as will mix it well together; stir it and beat it well up, and put it in a Dish to bake; put Puff-paste at the bottom of your Dish.

Eliza Smith's *The Compleat Housewife*, 1727

Some Yummy, Oldfashioned American Pies

~~~~~~

NESTLED in its puff paste, Eliza Smith's huge Carrot Pudding is actually, of course, what we call pie.

Pudding or pie, this is a delicious mixture which you can adapt easily to a more wieldable size. Try the following proportions in a seven-inch pie plate:

Line your pie plate with puff pastry; partly bake. In a basin mix this filling: 1 cup fine breadcrumbs, 1 grated, medium-size carrot, ½ cup wholegrain flour, 1 teaspoon cinnamon, ¼ nutmeg grated, a little salt (a few grains only), and ¼ cup oil or melted butter.

Mix in ¼ cup hot sherry, ¾ cup turbinado sugar, and 6 well-beaten eggs. Add enough cream (about ⅓ cup) to make a light mixture and beat well with an egg beater. Put the mixture into the crust. Mix a few breadcrumbs with a little sugar and sprinkle over the pie. Preheat the oven to 400°; after five minutes reduce to 325° and continue baking for twenty minutes.

As some scholars may know, sack was a generic term used in Merrie England to describe wines imported from Spain and the Canary Isles; the sack used by Mistress Smith would have been sherry.

More than a century later, Mrs. Henderson has some interesting comments on the subject of pie-making—including, incidentally, the nomenclature.

"I mean Yankee pies," says she, forthright as ever. "Our English cousins, when speaking of pies, mean only meat-pies, calling our pies tarts. When the paste is fitted over the pie-plate, cut round the edge of it with a sharp knife dipped in flour. Now cut a long curved strip, about three-quarters of an inch wide, wet slightly the top of the paste on the pie-plate near the edge (*not the edge*), and fit the strip around the pie, the edges coming together. Fill the pie, and place in the oven as soon as possible."

As you can see, the old-fashioned housewife-cooks— and the great chefs, too—took pride in pastry-making, creating the two basic pie crust mixtures (puff, and short) with equal ease.

My mother, who created the cakes for the teashop situated on the edge of London's Hampstead Heath which she owned with a friend, was renowned for her puff pastry. I recall her pies and tartlets as truly melting, and light as the puff-balls blown across the tough heath grasses.

The one ingredient essential to puff pastry—is no ingredient, but the coolness of your hands, and the temperature in the kitchen, which should be low, too. In fact, pastry is so affected by temperature that on a warm day my mother would wash her hands in cool water before working; in heat waves, she'd try to postpone her pastry-making.

If your kitchen, like my mother's, is without air conditioning, make a large quantity of pastry on a cool day, and freeze the part you don't use.

Marion Harland and Christine Terhune Herrick also stress the importance of a cool atmosphere, saying: "There must be good materials, a well-regulated oven, a cool room, and a cook who brings to her work a cool, light, quick hand, close attention, and a little experience. There are four principal kinds of pastry: puff paste; short crust, for family use; standing crust for meat and fish pies; and brioche paste, which is a sort of dough used for loaves, rolls, and buns...."

My mother's puff-paste mixture, however, which my father deemed so delicious, was similar to Miss Shute's:

Puff Paste

Miss Shute's *American Housewife*,
1879

"One pound of flour, one pound of butter, the
yolks of two eggs, mix with ice water. Mix half the
butter with the flour; stir the beaten yolks of the
eggs into a cupful of ice-water, or enough to make
into a dough; roll out the paste very thin, put the
butter on in layers, using about a third each time;
when it is all used up, roll up the paste and keep it in
a cool place."

Natural foods ingredients (for two nine-inch pies):

1 lb wholewheat pastry
   flour (fine grind)
pinch of sea salt

1 lb unsalted butter
2 yolks of fertilized eggs
1 c iced water

Marion Harland and Christine Terhune Herrick
come up with two easy-to-make recipes:

Pastry

Marion Harland and Christine
Herrick's *Modern Cooking*, 1904

"One heaping cup [wholewheat] flour; ¼ teaspoonful salt; ¼ teaspoonful baking powder; 2
tablespoonfuls shortening; ¼ cup or more cold water.

"Sift the flour, salt, and baking-powder into a
bowl; and rub in the shortening until the whole is
reduced to a fine powder. Mix with the cold water to
make a stiff dough. Scrape on a floured board, and
pat and roll into a circular shape to fit the plate. Fit it
loosely into the plate, allowing it to come a little
over the edge, since it shrinks when baked. This
makes two crusts for plates of ordinary size [i.e., 9-
inch plates]."

You can vary the texture and lightness of your
baked goodies by using different grinds of wholewheat flour. For a heavier, chewier texture, use regular wholegrain flour. Fine or pastry grind produces a
flour not unlike white flour in texture; use this grind
for puff paste and cakes, light and non-chewey. Medium grind, (midway between the two) is good for
bread-making, cookies, and short pastry; while wholegrain where you can see the specks of milled hull
makes delicious, close-textured bread—the "real," old-
fashioned wholegrain kind. (See directions for making
Eliza Smith's AN ORDINARY CAKE.)

❧

Two essentially American, old-fashioned desserts made with pastry are apple pie and strawberry shortcake.

I could choose no finer dish from our first All-American cookbook than Apple Pie, and if this recipe is any to go by, Amelia Simmons baked a real good one.

Beset by practical problems—she could barely read or write—Amelia rose from her downtrodden path to a minor fame (now major) which was nearly thwarted by one of the dirtiest tricks ever played on a naive, unsuspecting person. The printer who produced the book changed the recipes, an act which if undetected would have rendered valueless Amelia's little work. Fortunately, she caught the scurvy trick and put back many, but not all, of the directions in a list of errata understandably long for so slender a volume.

On a hunch I checked Apple Pie in this list, and sure enough, the directions for its puff paste had been sabotaged.

Apple Pie

Amelia Simmons's *American Cookery,*
1796

"Stew and strain the apples, to every three pints, grate the peel of a fresh lemon, add cinnamon, mace, rose-water and sugar to your taste—and bake in paste No. 3."

Paste No. 3

"To any quantity of flour, rub in three fourths of its weight of butter; [and of eggs—twelve per peck of flour—] rub in one third or half, and roll in the rest.

"*Erratum:* for 12 eggs read 6."

And the passing of time hasn't softened the impact of that last little notation.

Several decades later, Mrs. Henderson asked her friend Miss Amanda Newton for her favorite recipe for apple pie. Amanda, who like Amelia put her own special touch on simple foods, gave her this one:

A Plain Apple-Pie

Mrs. Henderson's *Practical Cooking*,
1876

"Slice pippin apples, and put them between two layers of pie-paste, with enough water to keep them moist. When they are baked, lift the crust carefully off with a knife, and put it aside; now mash the apples with a spoon, season them with plenty of sugar, butter, and grated nutmeg; replace the top crust and sprinkle sugar over it. These pies are especially nice when freshly made, then allowed to cool, and served with cream poured over each piece as it is cut, ready to be eaten.

"I think the flavor of the apple is better preserved in this manner than if the seasoning were cooked in it. However, many stew the apples first, before baking them in the pie."

For a nine- or ten-inch pie you'll need 3¾ cups cored, sliced apples. Bake in a hot oven (450°) for ten minutes, then at 350° for half an hour or so.

Miss Shute, however, glorifies her plain apple pie with custard:

Apple Custard Pie

Miss Shute's *American Housewife*, 1879

"Stew some [unpeeled] apples until so soft that they will rub through a sieve [or blend]. To a quart of the stewed apples, add two teacups of sugar, one pint of milk, half a cupful of butter, five eggs, season with grated lemon peel, and bake in puff paste like custards."

There's enough filling here for two pies. For half quantity, use 3 eggs.

Natural foods ingredients for two nine-inch pies:

1 qt (4 c) stewed apples
2 teacups (1½ c) turbinado sugar
1 pt milk
½ c butter or margarine
5 fertilized eggs
grated lemon peel
PUFF PASTE

❧

Grape Pie

Table Talk, 1901

"An oldfashioned way of making grape pie is to simply fill the under crust with whole grapes, then add a ½ cup of sugar and a ½ cup of molasses. The pie is then covered and baked for 35 minutes."

Simple and scrumptious; for non–sweet tooths, cut the sugar by half.

Natural foods ingredients:

1 lb green grapes
½ c turbinado sugar or less
½ c molasses
pastry for 9" pie (see PASTRY or SHORT-CAKE PASTRY)

❧

The *real* mince pie, of course, is made with minced (hence "mince") beef and dried fruit, with apples and citron, and is indeed a production. But this mock version is rich enough to carry the day, particularly if you add some chopped nuts, such as hazelnuts or walnuts.

Mock Mince Pie

365 Desserts, 1901

"Seed and chop 1 cup of raisins. Roll 2 round water-crackers until rather fine. Chip 2 oz. of citron, . . . and add ½ cup of currants. Mix all these ingredients together and add ¼ teaspoonful of salt, juice and rind of 1 lemon, ½ cup of sugar, ½ cup of cider, ⅔ cup of molasses, 1 egg well beaten, a teaspoonful of cinnamon, ¼ teaspoonful of [ground] cloves and a grating of nutmeg. Mix all well together and bake the same as mince pie."

In place of water crackers, you can use wholegrain breadcrumbs.

Natural foods ingredients for two nine-inch pies:

1 c monukka raisins
¼ c wholegrain bread-
  crumbs
2 oz citron
½ c currants
pinch sea salt
juice and rind of 1 lemon
½ c turbinado sugar
½ c apple cider

⅔ c molasses
1 fertilized egg, beaten
1 tsp cinnamon
¼ tsp ground cloves
a little nutmeg, grated
2 nine-inch pastry cases
  (see PUFF PASTE or
  PASTRY)

❧

Dried Peach Custard Pie

Table Talk, 1901

"Stew dried peaches until perfectly soft; stand aside to cool. When cold, beat with egg beater [or blend] until smooth and light, sweeten to taste. To every cup of this pulp add 1 egg well beaten and ½ cup of milk; beat all well together. Pour into pie tins, lined with a good plain paste. Bake in a quick oven 30 minutes."

For less stewing, soak the dried peaches in hot water overnight. Then cook in the same water, with enough added to cover.

Natural foods ingredients to make one nine-inch pie:

⅔ c sun-dried peaches ½ c fresh milk
turbinado sugar to taste pastry for nine-inch pie
 1 fertilized egg, beaten   tin (see PASTRY)

When's a pie not a pie? When it's Miss Shute's Pumpkin Pie, which she bakes *without* a crust. However, more conventional cooks can pile this delicious mixture into pastry crusts, and come up with a super-pie for Thanksgiving.

Pumpkin Pie

Miss Shute's *American Housewife*, 1879

"Take one pint of pumpkin that has been stewed soft and pressed through a colander [or blended], melt a quarter of a pound of butter in half a pint of warm milk, a quarter of a pound of sugar, stirring them well together; one pint of rich cream will be better than milk and butter; beat eight eggs very light and add to the other ingredients alternately with the pumpkin; then stir in a wine glass of rose water and two [wine] glasses of wine mixed together, a large teaspoonful of powered mace and cinnamon mixed, and a grated nutmeg. Having stirred the mixture very thoroughly, put into a buttered dish and bake."

This mixture is ample filling for a 9-inch pie crust.

When serving cold, add a glaze of ¼ cup honey mixed with ⅓ cup chopped pecan meats. Gilding the lily, but great at holiday time.

Natural foods ingredients to fill one nine-inch pie:

1 pt (2 c) stewed pumpkin

¼ lb (4 oz) butter or margarine

½ pt (1 c) milk

¼ lb (4 oz) turbinado sugar

8 fertilized eggs

1 wineglass (¼ c) rose water

2 wineglasses (½ c) sweet wine

½ tsp powdered mace

½ tsp cinnamon

1 nutmeg, grated

You can add:

1 pie crust (see PASTRY);
glaze of honey and pecans (see above);
1 pt heavy cream in place of milk and butter.

❧

Those culinary emperors of the glorious, feasting years of the late nineteenth century, Francatelli, Escoffier, and Filippini, titled their recipes as the mood took them, honoring alike dead kings, countries and small towns, opera singers, and with an eye to the main chance—their employers.

Thanks to Escoffier, Nellie Melba of the legendary voice is immortalized—as Pêches Melba, General Ulysses S. Grant by a long-forgotten pudding (Filippini's), and Alexander the Great by, of all things, black coffee—by Filippini again, who also pays his loyalty dues to the brothers Delmonico by naming chocolate biscuits "Marie Delmonico."

Britain, Florence, and Hollywood all get coolers (the liquid kind) from Filippini, and Florence Nightingale a kedgeree (Francatelli's), while Queen Victoria gets a number of odd-sounding recipes (such as Marrow Bone Toast), apparently invented by herself but documented by Francatelli, who dished them up. Filippini christens Tomato with Rice after some gentleman called Watson—not Sherlock Holmes's, and surely not IBM's.

But the most charming and appropriate title of all goes to Filippini's almond pie, which the great immigrant chef calls simply:

Pie à la Martha Washington

Filippini's *The Table*, 1889

"Peel [blanch] four ounces of almonds; put them in a mortar with two ounces of . . . sugar, then pound them thoroughly, adding gradually one raw egg. When well pounded, add two ounces more of . . . sugar, two ounces of melted fresh butter, half a gill of rum, half a saltspoonful of ground cinnamon, six drops of orange-flower water, and break in another egg. Pound the whole briskly for five minutes, then add two ounces of well-pounded macaroons, and mix again for two minutes more. Line a pie-plate [with PASTE FOR PIES], pour all the preparation over, cover, and bake (in a moderate oven for fifty minutes) ; when arranged on a dessert dish, decorate the top and sides artistically with two ounces of candied cherries, three ounces of pear, one of angelica, two of apricot, and two of pineapple, all the fruits being candied, then send to the table."

If you're too exhausted to cope with the candied-fruit decoration, sprinkle the pie with sugar after it's baked, and shove back into the oven for two minutes, or enough time for the sugar to melt (another Filippini inspiration).

Natural foods ingredients for one seven-inch pie:

4 oz almonds
2 oz turbinado sugar
   plus 2 oz
1 fertilized egg plus 1
2 oz sweet butter
½ gill (¼ c) rum
pinch ground cinnamon

6 drops orange-flower water
2 oz macaroons
pastry crusts (see PASTRY)
assorted candied fruits for decoration

You can add:

sugar glaze in place of decoration.

❧

These little tartlets are typical of those baked so successfully by my mother for her tearoom aficionados. Serve hot or cold, as dessert, or with tea brewed in your best silver pot.

Don't worry, however, if you lack this elegant receptacle used for nineteenth-century gracious tea-drinking—the tarts are excellent eating no matter how you serve them.

Incidentally, some people get confused between filberts and hazelnuts, which is not surprising. Botanically speaking, filberts are *Corylus Americana*, hazelnuts *Corylus rostrata*. To you and me, and countless other cooks, this means hazelnuts are large filberts.

Hazelnut Tarts

Table Talk (Philadelphia), 1901

"Chop one cup of hazelnuts very fine and pound to a paste. Add one-half a cup of powdered sugar, a pinch of cinnamon, one teaspoonful of lemon juice, ¼ of a cup of sherry or the same amount of orange juice. Mix well with the nut paste, then add 2 eggs beaten very light, without separating. Fill the tart molds lined with crusts, as for a fruit tart, and bake in a moderate oven 30 minutes. When cold put a tablespoonful of whipped cream on each tart and serve."

For molds, use muffin pans.

Natural foods ingredients to make two cups filling:

1 c hazelnuts
½ c turbinado sugar
pinch of ground cinnamon
1 tsp lemon juice
¼ c sherry *or* orange juice
whipped cream for decoration
2 fertilized eggs
pastry (see PUFF PASTE)

Who doesn't enjoy strawberry—or any other kind of shortcake. This version is unusual, being served as a large pie.

Short-Cake Paste

Marion Harland and Christine
Herrick's *Modern Cooking*, 1904

"Two cups [wholewheat] flour; ½ teaspoonful salt; ½ even teaspoonful soda, and 1 slightly rounded teaspoonful cream of tartar, or 2 teaspoonfuls baking powder; ½ cupful butter; 1 cupful sweet milk.

"Sift the salt, soda, cream-tartar (or baking powder), and flour together, and rub in the butter, keeping it as cold as possible. Stir in the milk to make a dough just soft enough to handle. Turn it on a floured board; divide the dough into halves and roll each piece out to fit a round tin plate. Bake at once, in a hot oven. When done, turn out each cake and lay it on the clean under-side of the baking tin. With a thin, sharp knife, split the cake evenly, and lay the bottom crust on a china plate. Butter each half. Lay partly mashed, sweetened strawberries, peaches, applesauce, stewed rhubarb, or any hot cooked fruit suitable for pies, on the under crust, lay the upper crust over it, and serve as a pie. Powdered sugar may be sifted over the top. If liked, it may be served with cream."

❧

Oldfashioned Puddings, Chock Full of Goodness

THE other day, foraging for antiques, I came across an oldtime steamer, the tiered kind that cooks three or four walloping puddings at once. And I realized that here was one gadget that's disappeared from the modern kitchen—indeed, it's no longer manufactured.

Yet the old-fashioned steamed or boiled puddings are easy to make, and nutritionally a sound idea. Most, however, are a meal in one slice, and thus incongruous today as dessert following a full meal. But as a wholesome followup to a light repast, they are both delicious and sensible.

Both pie and pudding making are akin to baking bread; all three conjure up that sense of merriment of medieval times, when a meal—accompanied by musicians and chorus of hungry hangers-on, with mine host and hostess heading the long table dressed to the teeth in glowing and bejeweled robes—was like nothing but a Broadway musical.

Later of course the noisy period of the Middle Ages calmed down, and mealtime became, like everything else under the Puritans, a serious business. Nevertheless, the Puritan table was always lavish, but with simple food which actually was pretty rich by today's standards.

How to make an old-fashioned pudding:

You can steam, boil, or bake your pudding. For *steamed puddings,* use a regular steamer made for the purpose, or improvise by putting the basin containing the pudding into a large covered pot, which will act as a steamer.

The pudding in its basin must be surrounded by

steam; so stand your pudding in a colander or atop an empty can. In all cases, regular steamer or improvised make-do, the lid of the outer container must fit tightly, so that no steam escapes.

Fill the basin with pudding only to the three-quarters mark. Cover the pudding with oiled wax paper. Put the basin with the pudding into the pot. Fill your steamer with boiling water to halfway up the basin; the water will evaporate as it boils, so check every so often and make up the amount lost in steam by adding more *boiling* water. As you see, the trick is to keep the water up to its original level, and continuously boiling.

You can also steam your pudding in the oven. To do this, prepare as above, but cover the pudding with two layers of oiled wax paper. Sprinkle cold water on the first layer; this will stop the top of the pudding from scorching, which it's prone to do.

Preheat the oven to 400°, stand the pudding in its basin in a pan filled with water 1″ deep. Reduce the oven heat to 350°.

Time is according to the size of the pudding. Those very rich, enormous plum puddings can take eight or nine hours to cook; but a little half-pounder takes only between 1¼ to 1½ hours.

To boil pudding, fill a basin with pudding *up to the brim;* cover with oiled wax paper and tie the whole thing up in a pudding cloth (a square of cotton or muslin), knotting the corners of fabric over the top of the pudding—quite loosely however, because the pudding will expand and take up more space. To lift the basin up, clutch it by its knot.

Immerse the pudding except for its end of cloth in a pot of cold water; cover with a tight lid. Bring the water to the boil, adding more *boiling* water as it evaporates.

To bake a pudding, pour the mixture into an oiled or buttered pan, and bake in the oven. The temperature, and timing, vary with the recipe.

❧

The puddings that follow are particularly easy to make, mostly using stale bread. A good point about the one below is that you can use two egg whites in place of one whole egg—a great way to use up leftover egg whites. A handy recipe indeed.

Half Hour Pudding

365 Desserts, 1901

"Boil 1½ pts. of milk, pour it over as many stale pieces of bread as it will soften; let it stand 10 minutes, and add 1 unbeaten egg, 1 tablespoonful of sugar, a little butter, salt and nutmeg, 1 teaspoonful of cream of tartar, ½ teaspoonful of soda; beat all well together and add the rest of the milk, then stir in ½ cup of currants dusted with a little flour. Pour into a buttered bowl and steam ½ hour. Serve with a sauce. It is very nice without the currants."

Natural foods ingredients to serve four generously:

1½ pts (3 c) milk
pieces of stale bread
  1 fertilized egg
  1 tbsp turbinado sugar
a little butter or
    margarine

pinch of sea salt
a little grated nutmeg
  1 tsp cream of tartar
½ tsp soda
½ c currants
a little wholewheat flour

You can add:

2 to 3 c Orange or Molasses Sauce;
2 egg whites in place of 1 whole egg;
2 tsp baking powder in place of the cream of tartar and soda.

❧

Subtitling his book *My Jolly Friend's Secret*, Dr. Lewis was a joyous person, witty and outgoing. His "Jolly Friend's Secret," as you may have guessed, is a strong digestion, a rare possession in those days of heavy eating.

Girls and women, tightlaced almost to suffocation, were particularly embarrassed by flatulence, for which he suggests violent slapping of the midriff. On a suitable occasion I tried pounding my middle—and yes, the doctor's idea worked well, at least on me. (Caution: check with your doctor before you experiment.)

In a slaphappy fashion, the doctor was a good natural-foods cook, although he occasionally leaves out an ingredient or two, as in the recipe below. But don't worry, the missing foods are put back in.

Apple Pudding

Dr. Dio Lewis's *Our Digestion*, 1872

"Place in the bottom of a buttered pudding-dish a layer of [tart] apples cut in quarters; pour over these a few spoonfuls of water; then a layer of fine breadcrumbs; and so alternate until the dish is full, finishing with a layer of crumbs; moisten the whole with a little water. Cover it with a plate and place it in the oven; bake an hour and a half; just before taking out, remove the plate, and let the top brown. Serve with this sauce:

"*Sauce:* One cup of sugar, one tablespoonful of butter, one tablespoonful of molasses, two-thirds of a pint of boiling water. Flavor to your taste with nutmeg or lemon."

Note: You may prefer to eliminate the sauce, and instead dot each layer of breadcrumbs with butter or margarine, and each layer of apples with a little sugar and/or molasses. Add the optional flavorings if you wish, but leave out the extra water.

Natural foods ingredients:

The pudding:

2 to 3 lb cooking apples, quartered	about ¼ c water about 1 c breadcrumbs

The sauce:

1 c turbinado sugar 1 tbsp butter or margarine 1 tbsp molasses	⅔ pt (1⅓ c) boiling water nutmeg *or* lemon to taste

You can add:

all the sauce ingredients except the water before baking; see note above.

Baked Apple Pudding

Dr. Dio Lewis's *Our Digestion*, 1872

". . . slice about three quarts good cooking apples,
mostly sweet; mix these with one pint Graham flour
and one pint corn-meal, one teacup of sugar, and
water enough to moisten the whole. Sprinkle a deep
pudding-dish with corn-meal and put in the fruit
dough, make a batter of one teacup each of corn-meal
and wheat-meal, a tablespoonful of sugar, and water
or milk, and spread over the top. Bake three hours."

Our charming doctor forgets the egg for the batter
—unless you'll settle for an unleavened, and rather
chewy, crust. If not, beat and add two eggs to the
batter mixture. Serve topped with yogurt.

*Natural foods ingredients to make one enormous pud-
ding or two large ones:*

3 qt (9) large red cooking apples	1 c turbinado sugar *plus* 1 tbsp
1 pt (2 c) wholewheat flour *plus* 1 c	water
1 pt (2 c) cornmeal *plus* 1 c	2 fertilized eggs
	a little milk

You can add:

wholewheat in place of Graham flour;
2 eggs the doctor forgot;
½ pt yogurt (for topping).

❧

Here's a *real* quickie—make it on the double.

Quick Pudding

Hugo Ziemann and Mrs. Gillette's
White House Cook Book, 1887

"Soak and split some crackers; lay the surface over with raisins and citron; put the halves together, tie them in a bag, and boil fifteen minutes in milk and water; delicious with rich sauce."

As an easy-to-fix alternative to "rich sauce" use a syrup of hot jam or jelly made by boiling up equal quantities of jam, water, and turbinado sugar; or pour over honey.

Natural foods ingredients:

pieces of wholegrain
   crackers or cookies,
   approx. ½ cup per
   person
raisins of equal quantity

2 or 3 pieces of citron,
   cut up
milk and water to cover
sauce or honey

No oldtime cookbook was complete without its selection of rice and tapioca puddings, usually tucked away under invalids' and children's cookery, and appropriately insipid.

To my mind, rice pudding can make a fabulous dessert, particularly when cooked slowly and lovingly, and flavored and decorated thoughtfully. Here are two rice puddings, and a tapioca "pud"—all delicious.

Boiled Rice Pudding

365 Desserts, 1901

"One fourth of a lb. of rice flour, rather more than a pint of milk, sugar to taste, 1 teaspoonful each of ground cinnamon and lemon [rind, grated]. Mix the rice flour with a little cold milk; pour upon it a pint of boiling milk, which has been flavored; sweeten to taste; boil gently until it thickens, stirring all the time; place in a mould till cold. Serve on a glass dish and ornament with raspberry preserve."

Or top with fresh strawberries, if possible, with leaves; or whole strawberries from a good, "natural" preserve.

Natural foods ingredients to serve four to six:

¼ lb natural brown rice flour	1 tsp ground cinnamon
1 pt (2 c) milk	1 tsp grated lemon rind
turbinado sugar to taste (about 1½–2 tbsp)	raspberry preserve

You can add:

strawberries, sliced, or whole with leaves on, or whole strawberries from preserve.

❧

The fig is a unique fruit—it's highly nutritious, containing high quantities of calcium, potassium, and magnesium, as well as phosphorus acid and a protein-decomposing ferment called papain. In fact, the beneficial qualities of this dried fruit are too numerous to list; let's just say that as dessert, or candy for kids, the fig can't be topped.

Fig Rice

Table Talk, 1901

"Boil 1 cup of rice in a large cup of water for 30 minutes, then drain it and turn into a colander. Stand it in the oven until the rice is . . . dry. Chop ½ a pound of figs quite fine; mix them carefully with the rice, not breaking the grains; stand in the colander over a saucepan of boiling water, cover it with a lid and steam slowly for 20 minutes [or until cooked]. The colander must not touch the water. Serve hot with sweetened cream."

Use a fine-mesh colander (see STEAMED PUDDINGS), or spread a layer of cheesecloth over a regular colander.

As natural-foods cooks know, natural brown rice takes about an hour to cook, from start to finish.

You can use sauce instead of cream; or sweeten the latter with honey.

Natural foods ingredients to serve four:

1 c natural brown rice	½ lb dried figs
1 large (1¼ c) water *plus* water for steaming	1 c cream, sweetened

You can add:

sweeten the cream with honey or molasses;
a sauce, such as ARROWROOT, in place of cream.

❧

Tapioca Pudding

Lafcadio Hearn's *La Cuisine Créole*,
1885

"Put a coffee-cup of tapioca (soak it well first)
into a pint and a half of milk, set it where it will get
hot slowly, take it off when it boils, and when cool
add four well-beaten eggs; flavor with lemon [rind]
and peach [preserve], sweeten it to taste, and bake for
an hour in a hot oven. If this is wanted for one person, take half the quantity of tapioca and milk."

The cook for that famous vegetarian, Bernard Shaw,
often served desserts topped with marzipan (an old-
style spread made of almonds—see ALMOND PASTE),
thus giving the doughty genius his quota of protein in
an unusual and delicious form.

Since most kids gobble their food, almonds should
be ground before being given to them. And as a general rule, serve almonds with an alkalizing fruit such
as raisins.

Pudding à la Zouave

Table Talk, 1901

"Blanch ½ lb. almonds, pound them in a mortar,
a few at a time, adding ½ lb. of butter; then add 4
well beaten eggs, ½ pt. milk, ½ pt. sugar, and a
(wine) glass of raisin wine. Mix this until it forms a
smooth paste, then stir in 1 lb. grated apples, these
ingredients being properly mingled, put it into a well
buttered mould and bake 1 hour. (Unmould to
serve.) The raisin wine is simply water in which
raisins have been steeped for two hours, then cover
and stand in a cool place 24 hours."

To reduce the richness use dried milk reconstituted in place of fresh, and margarine instead of butter.

When steeping the raisins, pour ¼ cup water into a bowl; add raisins until they pile up out of the water.

Natural foods ingredients to serve twelve or less:

½ lb almonds
½ lb butter or margarine
4 fertilized eggs, beaten
½ pt (1 c) milk
½ pt (1 c) turbinado
   sugar

1 wineglass (¼ c) raisin wine (see above)
1 lb apples, grated

You can add:

dried milk reconstituted in place of fresh;
soybean margarine in place of butter.

Finally, here are two plum puddings, one no doubt served to Queen Victoria, since it is the inspiration of chef Francatelli; the other comes from Lafcadio Hearn's *La Cuisine Créole*. The rich fruit of the royal dessert is mixed with apples, coriander seeds, and lemon peel, and Lafcadio's democratic mixture with ginger and orange peel; otherwise the recipes are similar, which seems to point a moral.

When we were children, my mother heralded the Christmas season by making several plum puddings, each with its unique ingredient well churned in—shiny sixpences specially gotten mint-new from the bank. Later, we suffered agonies eating the pudding, fearful of not getting the treasure coupled with the scary thought of swallowing it. I have yet to discover how my mother manipulated the positions of the silvery coins to turn up, one each to a serving. Later, one of these Christmas puddings, cashless, took a curtain call at Easter. Christmas pudding has the hibernating qualities of fruit cake; you can store it for months, and sometimes years, in a tightly closed tin.

If you don't feel like feeding posterity, however, you can easily break down the quantities in these two recipes. A few currants or raisins more or less will not unduly affect the flavor or texture.

One way of coping with leftover plum pudding—other than nibbling into it like candy, or serving it cold with a dollop of yogurt—is to combine it with vanilla ice cream (See EASY PLUM PUDDING ICE CREAM).

Plum Pudding

Francatelli's Cook's Guide, 1888

"Put the following ingredients into a basin:—three-quarters of a pound of raisins, a like quantity of currants, six ounces of candied mixed-peel, one pound of chopped beef suet, four ounces of chopped apples, one pound of flour, six ounces of breadcrumbs, half a pound of moist sugar, five eggs, half a pint of milk, a [wine] glass of brandy, half an ounce of pounded cloves, cinnamon, and grated nutmeg, and a few coriander seeds, a teaspoonful of salt, and some grated lemon-peel; mix thoroughly, and boil the pudding either in a cloth or in a basin, or a plain mould, for four hours and a half; and when done serve with whip sauce, No. 93. [No. 93 in the Cook's Guide is Almond Cream Sauce.]"

Chopped beef suet is used in steam puddings because the little chips of suet spread through the pudding imparting an even flavor throughout the mixture. However, you can easily and successfully substitute a lard-type vegetable shortening; my preference is for coconut oil, which is naturally of the right consistency. If you really want to simulate suet, grate in some coconut, but remember that by doing so you will add another flavor. This idea, however, is excellent for plainer puddings; the oil alone, of course, is flat-tasting and thus will not affect the combination of flavors created by Mr. Francatelli or Mr. Hearn.

Turn the mixture into three well-oiled molds, and either boil each for 1½ hours, or steam each for 4½ hours.

This makes a close-textured, rich plum pudding, traditional style, reminiscent of Charles Dickens and *The Christmas Carol.*

Natural foods ingredients for six pounds of pudding:

¾ lb monukka raisins
¾ lb currants
6 oz candied mixed peel
1 lb chopped beef suet
4 oz chopped apples
1 lb wholewheat flour
6 oz breadcrumbs
½ lb turbinado sugar, moistened
5 fertilized eggs

½ pt (1 c) milk
1 wineglass (¼ c) brandy
½ oz ground cloves
½ oz ground cinnamon
½ oz grated nutmeg
a few coriander seeds
1 tsp sea salt
rind of 1 lemon, grated

You can add:

2 c coconut oil in place of suet;
6 oz of citron in place of mixed peel;
1¼ c buttermilk or sour milk in place of brandy—and omit also the fresh milk.

೬

With more eggs, Lafcadio's pudding is lighter textured:

Christmas Plum Pudding

Lafcadio Hearn's *La Cuisine Créole*,
1885

"One pound and a half of raisins, half a pound of currants, three-quarters of a pound of bread-crumbs, half a pound of flour, three-quarters of a pound of beef-suet, nine eggs, one wineglass of brandy, half a pound of citron and orange-peel, half a nutmeg, and a little ground ginger. Chop the suet as fine as possible, and mix it with the bread-crumbs and flour, add the currants, . . . the citron and orange-peel cut into thin slices, and the raisins stoned and divided. Mix it all well together with the grated nutmeg and ginger, then stir in nine eggs well beaten, and the brandy, and again mix it thoroughly together, that every ingredient may be moistened; put it into a buttered mould, tie it over tightly, and boil it for six hours. . . ."

Natural foods ingredients for six pounds or more of pudding:

1½ lb monukka raisins	½ lb (1 c) chopped citron
½ lb currants	
¾ lb breadcrumbs	½ lb (1 c) chopped orange peel
½ lb wholewheat flour	
¾ lb beef suet	½ nutmeg, grated
9 fertilized eggs	a little (2 tsp) ground ginger
1 wineglass (¼ c) brandy	

You can add:

1½ cups coconut oil in place of beef suet;
¼ cup buttermilk in place of brandy, or juice of 1½ lemons.

❦

And finally, here's Amelia Simmons's Carrot Pudding, rich with eggs and butter, but no cream.

Amelia, who surely possessed a fine figure, eschews cream in puddings, saying: "In all puddings, where cream is mentioned, milk may be used." She also has the right advice on cooking vegetables—advice that went unheeded until the present day. Referring to green beans, she says: "They will be soon done, make them boil quick."

Carrot Pudding

Amelia Simmons's *American Cookery,*
1796

"A coffee cup full of boiled and strained carrots, 5 eggs, 2 ounces sugar and butter each, cinnamon and rosewater to your taste, baked in a deep dish without paste."

Make your rosewater with milk, using about ¾ cup; this will improve the texture of the pudding. Beat well.

Natural foods ingredients:

1 c boiled carrots
5 fertilized eggs
2 oz turbinado sugar

2 oz butter
cinnamon and rosewater
   to taste

You can add:

¾ c milk;
honey in place of sugar.

Custards, Fools and Other Sweet Goodies

~~~~~~

CUSTARDS and fruit fools were popular sweets with oldtime chefs, thus Eliza Smith, Mrs. Rundell, and other cooks of the early days kept their desserts simple. But those enthusiastic housewives of the age of ruthless ornamentation turned plain food into decorative masterpieces reminiscent of those porcelain flower pieces set under glass, commemorating Victorian dear-departeds. Indeed, crystallized violets, rose petals, and sugary-green angelica all played their part atop cakes and desserts of all flavors, shapes, and sizes.

Today, these sugary goodies à la Escoffier may delight the eye, but are apt to sour stomachs used to simpler, more healthful fare. Yet stripped of their rich, nonnutritional nonsense, many desserts from those days are basically good eating, and many feature unusual ideas. Almond Custard, for instance, is a delicious dessert easy to make, yet I'm sure if fixed by Escoffier it would tower several inches in thick whipped cream, laced with liqueur brandy.

Custard can play it sweet or savory, and both ways are basically the same, except of course for the addition of flavorings. So here are hints for making the perfect basic custard:

Hints on Cooking Custard

For a smooth consistency, use 2 eggs for each cup of milk, and cook slowly.

For a combination that sets firmly in a shorter time, use 1½ eggs per 1 cup of milk.

Cook all kinds of custards over hot water, either set in a pan in the oven heated to 325° to 350°, or in a double boiler.

When making *custard pies,* combine the eggs with *boiling* milk; this sets the eggs quickly, and keeps the bottom crisp.

Always make a *boiled custard* in a double boiler, and stir the mixture constantly with an egg whisk. For extra smoothness, pour into a cocktail shaker and go to it, as for a cocktail.

A fraction, and I mean fraction, (too much tastes awful) of a pinch of salt gives zip to custard's normally bland flavor.

For *baked custards:* If the custard's to be served, browned, in its dish, beat the mixture hard before cooking. If baked in a mold, to be turned out, go easy on the beating.

A nice touch for sweet custard: sprinkle with grated nutmeg before baking.

Orange Custard

Table Talk, 1901

"Scald 1 pint of milk. Beat the yolks of 3 eggs light with ¼ of a cup of sugar. Slowly pour the milk on the eggs beating all the while, and when well mixed put back into the farina [double] boiler with chippings of the rind of the orange. Cook for 2 minutes or until smooth and thick, stirring constantly. Add the juice of two oranges, strain and put away to cool."

Caution: Don't add the orange juice until the custard's cool.

Natural foods ingredients to serve four:

1 pt (2 c) fresh milk   ¼ c turbinado sugar
3 fertilized egg yolks   2 oranges

You can add:

⅓ c honey in place of sugar.

Strawberries are truly old-fashioned fruit. Shake-speare mentions them, and they appear often in Medieval writings. In fact, the French author, Fontenelle, swore he owed his long life—he passed the century mark—to the healing properties of strawberries. Who knows—he may have been right; strawberries are high in vitamin C.

Strawberry Custard

Table Talk, 1901

"Separate four eggs, put one pint of milk into a double boiler, beat the yolks of the eggs and four tablespoonfuls of sugar until light; add them to the milk; stir constantly until the thickness of cream, take from the fire and stand aside to cool; beat the whites of the eggs until stiff, add to them four tablespoonfuls of . . . sugar and beat again until stiff and white. Put about a pint of strawberries into a glass dish, pour over the custard, heap the whites in spoonfuls over the top, dust with sugar, stand in the oven a minute to brown. Serve icy cold."

Natural foods ingredients to serve four:

4 fertilized eggs   1 pt (2 c) strawberries
1 pt (2 c) fresh milk
4 tbsp turbinado sugar
  plus 4 tbsp and a little

Coconut Pudding

365 Desserts, 1901

"One quart of milk, half a coconut grated, 4 eggs, a little salt and sugar to taste. Bake in a quick oven about 30 minutes. Serve with sauce [ARROWROOT or ORANGE]."

❧

Almond Custard

Miss Shute's *American Housewife*,
1879

"Scald a pint of rich milk; stir it gradually on to three well-beaten eggs, four tablespoonfuls of sugar, four ounces of almonds, blanched and pounded to a paste, a few at a time in a mortar [or pulverized in an electric grinder], and mixed with two tablespoonfuls of rose water, or orange flower water, and a little salt. Return it to the fire and boil a few minutes, stirring it constantly until it thickens. Turn it into a pitcher, and when nearly cold fill the cups. Make a meringue of the whites of two eggs and two tablespoonfuls of powdered sugar; flavor with a teaspoonful of extract of . . . almonds."

Instead of meringue (made with white sugar) decorate with chopped almonds, lightly toasted. Or top with a blob of yogurt.

To make Orange-flower or Rose Water: Mix a few drops of orange or rose essence into a tablespoon of water. It should be distilled water; however, ordinary spring or tap water will do.

Natural foods ingredients to serve six to eight:

The custard

1 pt (2 c) fresh milk
3 fertilized eggs, beaten
4 tbsp turbinado sugar
4 oz ground almonds
  (see above)

2 tbsp orangeflower or
  rose water
a little sea salt

For the meringue (optional):

whites of 2 fertilized eggs
2 tbsp powdered sugar

1 tsp almond extract

You can add:

in place of meringue, decorate with dollops of yogurt
or toasted, chopped almonds.

Mrs. Henderson, with a nineteenth-century eye for
the decorative table, has some great ideas for serving
fresh fruit, which she says she acquired from the
French. Her comments are illustrated with charming
engravings, which I will try to re-create verbally, a
difficult task.

How to Serve Fruits

Miss Parloa's *New Cook Book*, 1880

"The French deserve much praise for their taste in
arranging fruits for the table. They almost invariably
serve them with leaves, even resorting to artificial ones
in winter.

"In the following arrangements, I have some of
their dainty dishes in mind."

Strawberries

"The French serve large fine strawberries without being hulled. Pulverized sugar is passed, the strawberry is taken by the thumb and finger by the hull, dipped into the sugar, and eaten. . . .

Grapes

"Always choose a raised dish for fruits. Arrange part of the clusters of grapes to fall gracefully over the edge of the dish. Mix any kind of pretty green leaves or vines, which may also fall, and wind around the stem of the dish. Although the colors of the fruits should blend harmoniously, and the general appearance should be fresh and *negligé,* arrange them firmly, so that when the dish is moved there will be no danger of an avalanche."

Mrs. Henderson sounds like she knows whereof she speaks.

Cantaloupe Melons

"Put it into the refrigerator until just before serving, to become thoroughly chilled; cut it as in figure here given, removing the seeds. Arrange four or five grape leaves on a platter, upon which place the melon."

Her illustration shows a delicately engraved melon, sliced downwards like a giant radish, the base being uncut and solid, so that the pieces can be pulled back, forming a "water lily." Frankly, it's a beautiful way to serve a melon, and if you can't find vine leaves, decorate your lily-melon platter with large, dark celery leaves.

And here's another lovely idea from the imaginative talent of Mrs. Henderson:

Currants

"Serve currants in rows of red and white, with a border of leaves around the outside. . . ."

A great idea, too, for a pile-up of monukka raisins and sunflower seeds. Border the bowl with leaves; fill it with raisins (separated), then depress a hole in the center. Fill up with sunflower seeds.

Incidentally this, and other ideas above, make good centerpieces. Demolish as the final course.

Huckleberries with Crackers and Cream

Hugo Ziemann and Mrs. Gilette's
White House Cook Book, 1887

"Pick over carefully one quart of blueberries, and keep them on ice until wanted. Put into each bowl, for each guest, two soda crackers, broken in not too small pieces; add a few tablespoonfuls of berries, a teaspoonful of powdered sugar, and fill the bowl with the richest of cold, sweet cream. This is an old-fashioned New England breakfast dish. It also answers for a dessert."

I've made this dish many times, not realizing I'd re-created a New England recipe. As a variation on Mrs. Gillette's, try cake or wholegrain bread in place of soda crackers, and honey in place of sugar.

Incidentally, Mrs. Gillette is not confused—huckleberries are similar to blueberries, but darker and with more seeds. The choice is yours.

Finally, yogurt or buttermilk make delicious substitutes for cream—the slightly tangy flavor of each goes well with the fruit.

Natural foods ingredients for each bowlful:

½ c blueberries	1 tbsp turbinado sugar
2 crackers	¼ c cream

You can add:

yogurt or buttermilk in place of cream;
honey in place of sugar;
cake or cookies in place of crackers—or even wholegrain bread.

❧

Huckleberry Shortcake

Table Talk, 1901

"Beat 2 tablespoonfuls butter to a cream with ½
cup of sugar; add 1 egg unbeaten, and beat the mixture very light; add 4 tablespoonfuls of milk and ¾
cup of flour, to which has been [sifted in] 1 teaspoonful of baking powder; mix quickly and lightly.
Bake in [2] well greased, deep pie-plates for 20 minutes in a moderate oven. The berries must be slightly
cooked with a little sugar to start the juice, then
spread on the cake."

For Strawberry Shortcake, use fresh, ripe strawberries in place of huckleberries.

Natural foods ingredients to make six small shortcakes:

2 tbsp butter or
  margarine
	¾ c wholewheat flour,
	  pastry grind

½ c turbinado sugar	1 tsp baking powder
1 fertilized egg	
4 tbsp milk, fresh or dried reconstituted	

❧

Fools, flummeries, and syllabubs—we still make these age-old dishes with musical names.

Originally a mixture of cream and fresh fruit, fool is now usually made with custard. Eliza Smith's oldtime recipe, however, still ranks tops. She suggests you "Take a pint of Raspberries; squeeze and strain the Juice with Orange-flower-water; put to the Juice five ounces of fine Sugar; then set a pint of Cream over the Fire, and let it boil up; then put in the Juice, give it one stir around, and then put it in your Basin; stir it a little in the Basin, and when 'tis cold use it."

Flummery is fool made with a gruel (i.e., cereal) base instead of cream, while syllabub is a drink made of milk curdled with an acid such as cider or wine. (Eliza Smith's syllabub is made with cream curdled with lemon juice, then "whipt.")

You can use any kind of soft, stewed fruit in the following recipe:

Apricot Fool

Table Talk, 1901

"Soak ½ a lb. of [sun-dried] apricots overnight. In the morning put them in a porcelain-lined [enamel or stainless steel] kettle with sufficient water to cover. Cover the kettle and stew slowly until tender; then [blend] till smooth and entirely free from lumps. Add 1 tablespoonful of butter, yolks of 4 eggs well beaten, and a ½ cup of sugar. Beat the whole until thoroughly mixed; and pour into a glass dish. [Meringue:] Beat the whites of the eggs until light; add two heaping tablespoonfuls of powdered sugar, mixing thoroughly; heap on top of the apricots and stand away until cold."

In place of meringue, top with yogurt. Or serve as is, with no topping.

Natural foods ingredients to serve six:
For the Fool:

½ lb (sun-dried) apricots	4 fertilized egg yolks,
1 tbsp butter or	beaten
margarine	½ c turbinado sugar

For the Meringue:

white of the 4 eggs	½ c sugar

You can add:

dollops of yogurt in place of meringue.

Strawberry Flummery

Table Talk, 1901

"Place one quart of strawberries in a farina [double] boiler, allow them to heat just a little while until the juice flows freely. Have ready two table-spoonfuls of cornstarch, moistened in a gill of cold water; add to the berries one pint of boiling water and a cup of sugar; stir in the cornstarch, stir rapidly for a moment and turn into a mould. Serve icy cold with whipped cream."

Natural foods ingredients to serve six to eight:

2 boxes strawberries	1 pt (2 c) water, boiling
(about 2 lbs)	1 c turbinado sugar
2 tbsp cornstarch	1 c heavy cream,
1 gill (½ c) water	whipped

Potatoes for dessert? Why not? Furthermore, this is a good way of using leftover mashed ones, if unpeppered (lightly salted's okay).

Potato Rolls for Dessert

Table Talk, 1901

"Put 2 cups of mashed potatoes in the Keystone beater; add ½ cup sugar, yolks of 2 eggs, tablespoonful of butter, ½ nutmeg grated, ½ teaspoonful cinnamon. Beat till the whole is thoroughly mixed and very light. Form in cylindrical shaped rolls; dip in egg and then in bread crumbs, and fry in smoking hot fat. Serve hot with vanilla sauce.

"*Vanilla Sauce:* Put ½ pt. milk in a double boiler to boil. Beat the yolks of 4 eggs with 2 tablespoonfuls sugar until very light; then add them to the scalding milk; stir over the fire one minute, turn out to cool; add a teaspoonful vanilla, mix and stand away until very cool."

For "Keystone beater" read "regular mixer"—unless your grandmother can lend you the former.

Natural foods ingredients to make about six rolls:

2 c cooked, mashed potatoes
½ c turbinado sugar
2 fertilized egg yolks *plus* 1 egg
1 tbsp butter or margarine

½ whole nutmeg, grated
½ tsp ground cinnamon
½ c breadcrumbs
oil for frying

Vanilla sauce:

½ pt (1 c) milk, fresh
4 fertilized egg yolks

2 tbsp turbinado sugar
1 tsp real vanilla extract

You can add:

vanilla pod to the sauce in place of essence. Use the whole pod; remove before serving, rinse under the faucet, and store away for another time. The pod keeps its flavor through several cookings. Store in sugar to make *Vanilla Sugar*—and use the pod as above.

∿

Here's a simple, delicious, and easy-to-fix fruit-jelly dessert you can make with agar-agar or carrageen moss. It's excellent, too, made with honey.

Orange Sponge

365 Desserts, 1901

"1 oz. gelatine [cooked] in 1 qt. water; strain and stand until it begins to thicken, then add whites of 3 eggs, the juice of 2 lemons and 1 large orange. Sweeten to the taste, beat all thoroughly and put in moulds."

In place of gelatine prepare carrageen moss according to directions on the packet to make one quart jelly. Let stand to thicken, then proceed as above, adding the whites of three eggs, as directed. Serve unmolded, topped with yogurt.

Natural foods ingredients to serve four to six:

1 oz gelatine	juice of 2 lemons
1 qt water	1 large orange
whites of 3 fertilized eggs	turbinado sugar to taste

You can add:

carrageen moss in place of gelatine;
yogurt for topping;
honey in place of sugar.

∿

7

Really Great, Oldfashioned Ice Cream

To make Pistachia Cream.

PILL your Pistachias, and beat them very fine, and boil them in Cream; if 'tis not green enough, add a little Juice of Spinage; thicken it with Eggs, and sweeten to your Taste; pour it in Basons, and set it by till 'tis cold.

Eliza Smith's *The Compleat Housewife*, 1727

"I scream, you scream
We all scream
For ICE CREAM"
Kids' song from way back.

Eliza Smith, like many oldtime cookbook authors, writes as she speaks. So she "pills" her "pistachias" instead of peeling, or shelling them. Otherwise, you can follow her recipe for your own Pistachio Ice Cream, using one of the basic ice cream recipes which follow. For the only difference in method between Eliza Smith's Pistachia Cream and the Baskin-Robbins stuff is the freezing.

Ice cream has been around a long, long time. Way back in Poland it was a popular dessert, the cream being frozen like a brick in the bottom of the deep well situated on every nobleman's estate; water ices were popular in China at least a thousand years before Christ. Somewhere along the line, the recipe reached the Italian cooks of the Renaissance, and they in turn gave the idea to the French (along with other delicacies that make up French cuisine).

More recently, Thomas Jefferson, an ice-cream lover, and one of the world's great gourmets, often served the creamy dessert to his guests at the White House, taking particular pleasure in vanilla; indeed, he was responsible for the present-day French ice cream,* a rich and heady mixture the recipe for which he brought over from France, together with several hundred vanilla beans.†

But—Women's Libbers, note—it was an American housewife, one Nancy Johnson, who in 1848 came up

---

* You can make a version of Thomas Jefferson's French Ice Cream from his recipe featured in Mrs. Helen Duprey Bullock's *The Thomas Jefferson Cookbook*.

† Mrs. Helen Bullock is preparing a new edition of Thomas Jefferson's cookbook.

with that brilliant culinary invention, the freezing machine, complete with hand crank. And like the modern sewing machine, which in essence is the same as Mr. Singer's original, today's ice-cream freezer works on the principle created by Ms. Johnson. (Electricity of course merely takes the place of your elbow grease.)

Then, too, whether you're handcranking at a picnic, or plugging your freezing machine into a wall socket in the kitchen, your ice cream mixture is basically the same as that used by Filippini, or by Eliza Smith for her cold dessert—which she would no doubt have frozen down the family well, had it been icy enough.

All the same, although the oldtime favorites—vanilla and chocolate—have lasted through the decades, other flavors typical of the period have come and gone. What, for instance, could be more *fin de siècle* than banquet-rich Plum Pudding Ice Cream, or more Victorian domestic than Brown Bread Ice Cream—both delicious and well worth reviving, particularly the latter in these days of high food prices.

Your Freezing Machine and How to Use It:

Ice cream depends for its delectability on texture as much as flavor, hence the need to churn the mixture as it freezes.

The *ice cream machine* is a simple contraption consisting of a bucket, preferably wooden, in the center of which is placed a metal container holding the ice-cream mixture. Next, the dasher, a kind of cut-up spade, now usually made of plastic, is set in the middle of the mixture and held in place by the lid which is clamped over the container.

In the top of the lid is a socket which holds the hand crank or electric motor. This is a separate, removable piece which sits astride the top of the bucket and is fixed to either side of its outer edge. When the crank is turned in a circle, it moves the bucket containing the mixture (not the dasher, as you might expect). This circular motion, of course, churns the ice cream as it is frozen by the shaved ice packed around the bucket.

After about twenty-five minutes of personal or electric churning, your mixture will have become a mushy mess, delicious to the taste buds but not yet ice cream; this mush has to be hardened, either in the freezing machine, or in the freezing compartment of the refrigerator. If the latter, re-pot into plastic containers; switch temperature to coldest.

To harden in the freezing machine: pile more ice and salt around the metal container; place some newspaper or a piece of aluminum foil over the lid of the container (remember, you've removed the crank and motor) and pile ice on that, so that the container holding the mixture is packed within ice and salt. Hardening (or ripening, as it's sometimes called) by this method takes two to three hours, during which time you pile on more ice and salt as it melts away. The water drains off through a hole in the side of the bucket.

Traditionally, there are *three basic types of ice-cream mixtures,* and a fourth, *the water ice,* which of course is not made with cream. Your choice, therefore, lies between *French,* which is a rich custard made with egg yolks and heavy cream; *American,* or *mousse-style,* which is also a custard but with a stabilizer such as arrowroot or rice added to prevent ice crystals from hugging each other; and lastly, *Philadelphia style,* which contains no eggs, but only cream and flavoring and, of course, sugar or honey.

All the ice-cream recipes given will work beautifully in a modern electric freezer. So whirl away, and send up thanks to Ms. Johnson for her fine invention.

Alessandro Filippini gives us this simple recipe for Vanilla Ice Cream. Study his meticulously clear instructions and use the recipe as a basis for other flavors.

Vanilla Ice Cream

Fillippini's *The Table*, 1889

"Boil in a saucepan one pint of milk with half a vanilla bean [pod]; put in a vessel half a pound of . . . sugar, and six egg yolks, and with a spatula mix thoroughly for ten minutes; then add it to the boiling milk, stirring for two minutes longer, and pour the whole into a . . . saucepan, placing it on a moderate stove to heat for five minutes, stirring at the bottom continually with the spatula, and being careful not to let it boil. Remove from off the fire, place it on a table, [take out the vanilla pod] and add immediately one pint of sweet cream, still mixing it for two minutes more; let cool off for thirty minutes, then strain through a sieve into an ice-cream freezer; put on the lid, and lay it in an ice-cream tub, filling the freezer all around with broken ice, mixed slightly with rock salt; then turn the handle on the cover as briskly as possible for three minutes. Lift up the lid, and with a wooden spoon detach the cream from all around the freezer, and the bottom as well. Re-cover it, and turn the handle sharply for three minutes more; uncover, and detach the cream the same as before, being careful that no ice or salt drops in. Put the lid on, and repeat the same three times more. The ice-cream should by this time be quite firm, so have a cold dessert-dish with a folded napkin, dress the ice-cream over, and send to the table.

This same ice-cream can be formed into a single brick by having a brick-shaped form, filling it with the cream, and pressing it down quickly with a spoon. . . ."

You can also harden the ice cream in the refrigerator, as described previously.

Natural foods ingredients to make about one gallon:

1 pt (2 c) milk, fresh   6 fertilized egg yolks
half a vanilla pod   1 pt (2 c) heavy cream
½ lb turbinado sugar

∾

From the sublime to the simple; an ice cream made American style—with arrowroot, and without cream. Use it in place of the richer ice creams, flavoring in the same manner with vanilla, chocolate, etc.

Another Mode of Ice Cream

Miss Shute's *American Housewife,*
1879

"Mix four teaspoonfuls of arrow-root . . . with a little milk; boil two quarts of milk, and stir the arrow-root into it; let it boil until it begins to thicken; then add two quarts of cold milk, three pounds of sugar and flavoring to taste."

These quantities call for a 6-quart freezer; alternatively, reduce the amounts, and if small, refrigerate until solid (2 hours) in the freezer tray of the refrigerator, hand stirring the mixture first, and again when it's become a firm mush.

Flavor with chopped nuts, dates (reduce the quantity of sugar), vanilla pod or extract, almonds, etc. Chips of ginger root are good.

Natural foods ingredients to make one and one-half gallons (six quarts):

4 tsp arrowroot   3 lb turbinado sugar
2 qt milk *plus* 2 qt *plus*   flavoring (see above)
a little

∾

For sheer simplicity, Mrs. Gillette's recipe is hard to beat:

Pure Ice Cream

Hugo Ziemann and Mrs. Gillette's
White House Cook Book, 1887

"Genuine ice cream is made of the pure sweet cream in this proportion: Two quarts of cream, one pound of sugar; beat up, flavor and freeze.

"For family use, select one of the new patent freezers, as being more rapid and less laborious for small quantities than the old style turned entirely by hand. All conditions being perfect, those with crank and revolving dashers effect freezing in eight to fifteen minutes."

Very simple—and very rich. Flavor with vanilla pod for the real McCoy.

～

Chocolate Ice Cream No. 1
(Very Fine)

Hugo Ziemann and Mrs. Gillette's
White House Cook Book, 1887

"Add four ounces of grated chocolate to a cupful of sweet milk, then mix it thoroughly to a quart of thick, sweet cream; no flavoring is required but vanilla. Sweeten with a cupful of sugar; beat again and freeze."

Natural foods ingredients to make two quarts ice cream:

4 oz chocolate	vanilla pod or essence to
1 c sweet milk	taste
1 qt heavy cream	1 c turbinado sugar

You can add:

carob in place of chocolate.

❧

Coconut Ice Cream

Hugo Ziemann and Mrs. Gillette's
White House Cook Book, 1887

"One quart of cream, one pint of milk, three eggs, one cupful and a half of sugar and one of prepared [grated fresh] coconut, the rind and juice of a lemon. Beat together the eggs and grated lemon-rind, and put with the milk in the double boiler. Stir until the mixture begins to thicken. Add the coconut and put away to cool. When cool, add the sugar, lemon-juice and cream. Freeze."

Natural foods ingredients to make two quarts and some over:

1 qt heavy cream	1½ c turbinado sugar
1 pt (2 c) milk	1 c coconut, grated
3 fertilized eggs	1 lemon, rind and juice

You can add:

dried milk reconstituted in place of fresh.

❧

Fruit Cream

Hugo Ziemann and Mrs. Gillette's
White House Cook Book, 1887

"Make a rich, boiled custard; flavor with wine and vanilla and pour into a freezer. When half frozen, add pounded almonds, chopped citron and brandy, [fresh] peaches or chopped raisins. Have the freezer half full of custard and fill up with the fruit. Mix well, and freeze again. Almost any kind of fruits that are preferred may be substituted for the above."

Use the custard from COCONUT ICE CREAM as a base.

Fruit Ice Cream

Hugo Ziemann and Mrs. Gillette's
White House Cook Book, 1887

"*Ingredients*—To every pint of fruit juice allow one pint of cream; sugar to taste.

"Let the fruit be well ripened; pick it off the stalks, and put it into a large earthen pan. Stir it about with a wooden spoon, breaking it until it is well-mashed; then, with the back of the spoon, rub it through a hair-sieve [i.e. a fine sieve]. Sweeten it nicely with pounded sugar; whip the cream for a few minutes, add it to the fruit, and whisk the whole again for another five minutes. Put the mixture into the freezer and freeze. Raspberry, strawberry, currant, and all fruit ice-creams are made in the same manner. A little pounded sugar sprinkled over the fruit before it is mashed assists to extract the juice. In winter, when fresh fruit is not obtainable, a little [strawberry] jam may be substituted for it; it should be melted and worked through a sieve before being added to the whipped cream.

"In making berry flavoring ice-cream, the milk should never be heated; the juice of the berries added to *cold* cream, or fresh, rich milk, mixed with *cold* cream, the juice put in just before freezing, or when partly frozen."

To make a more nutritious—and delicious—ice cream, add some of the fruit pulp, with honey in place of sugar.

Natural foods ingredients:

fruit juice, any kind, *plus*   equal quantity of cream
    some pulp   sugar or honey to taste

You can add:

half honey in place of half the sugar;
fruit pulp.

∽

If you love bread-and-butter pudding (to my mind one of the simpler joys of life), this ice cream is for you; it's a frozen version of that delectable dessert.

In most antique cookbooks stale bread is featured as a regular ingredient, often in ice-cream recipes similar to this one.

Brown Bread Ice Cream

Marion Harland and Christine
Herrick's *Modern Cooking*, 1904

"Stale bread must be used for this cream, mixed with an equal quantity of stale sponge cake. Take 2 sponge cakes and 2 thick slices of bread, grate them into a jug, and pour over ½ pint of milk, and 1 pint of cream, made sweet with ½ pound of sugar. Place the jug in a saucepan, and stir the contents over the fire until it gets thick. A few of the bread crumbs sifted very finely may be added with a [wine] glass of any . . . liqueur liked to the mixture when quite cold, and just before being put to freeze. Freeze for about twenty-five minutes."

We tried this ice cream with stale bread, wholegrain of course, and with carrot cake. In each case it was delicious, flavored either with apple cider or sherry wine, and frozen in the refrigerator.

Natural foods ingredients to make about two quarts:

2 thick slices wholegrain bread and equal amount of stale cake
½ pt (1 c) milk, fresh or dried reconstituted
1 pt (2 c) cream

½ lb turbinado sugar or less
1 wineglass (¼ c) any liqueur liked such as Drambuie or Kirsch

You can add:

sherry or apple cider in place of liqueur.

When we were kids, my sister and I spent our summers in a several-centuries-old cottage in East Bergholt in England. This is "Constable country," and our cottage (now under the jurisdiction of the British National Trust) had been featured by the great landscape painter in one of his paintings of this pretty village.

It was here in the lavender-scented garden that my mother made delicious ice cream in an ancient freezer, which my sister and I took turns to crank; and I assure you there's no greater joy than licking a cone-full of ice cream you've cranked yourself, with great enthusiasm.

The cottage was a typical, country-folks' home with minuscule rooms; there really were roses around its door (actually, at the tiny garden gate) and honeysuckle entwining the lintel, and of course it was crowned with a thatched roof where birds nested. They'd wake us at dawn, chattering and peeking in at the little bedroom windows set under the overlapping thatch.

The kitchen was cobblestoned, with a "copper" (a large copper tub with a chimney breaking through its center to take off the smoke from the fire underneath which supplied the heat) where clothes and small children were dunked. The cottage had not been modernized, and all its furnishings—sink, cupboards, and huge black range set alongside one wall—were at least a couple of hundred years old. The soft, caressing light was by candle or oil lamps; but we bedded at dusk, in cold weather snuggled under eiderdown quilts (only the eider duck can provide such cuddlesome warmth—he parts with the soft down from under his breast). And of course, we all braved the darkness of surrounding trees when we ran down to the "john" at the far end of the garden.

It was a romantic little structure, picturesque, homey with animals—dogs, cats, geese and my own pet hen, Helen—wandering through the back door of the kitchen, hoping for a tidbit, and being shooed right out. These forays were always noted enviously by the goat tethered to a tree nearby, his beard giving him a professorial look he didn't merit. Actually, you had to watch him for he spent his day waiting for your rear end to come within reach of his sharp little horns —then down went his head, and ouch. It was his one big joke.

The ice cream my mother used to make at the cottage was created with a simple cream or custard base, to which she added different flavors, many similar to the following.

To your favorite ice-cream base add the ingredients listed to make:

Maple Ice Cream:

Add 1 cup maple syrup to each 4 cups of cream. Pour over Maple Sauce, i.e. ARROWROOT SAUCE and maple syrup heated together in equal quantities.

Peach Ice Cream:

Add 2 cups stewed peaches blended to pulp and 1 teaspoon lemon juice to each 4 cups cream used.

Wine Ice Cream:

Add 2 teaspoons sherry or Madeira to each 4 cups cream used. (Good too, with Japanese plum wine.)

Ginger Ice Cream:

Add one cup preserved ginger chopped fine, two tablespoons lemon juice, and three tablespoons ginger syrup.

Nougat Ice Cream:

Add one ½ cup each of walnuts, almonds, and filberts, chopped, together with 1 teaspoon each real vanilla and almond extracts for each 4 cups of base.

Almond/Pistachio Ice Cream:

Add ½ cup pistachio nuts and one cup almonds, both chopped fine; also 1 teaspoon almond extract for each 4 cups cream used. Color pistachio with natural food coloring. (See Eliza Smith's PISTACHIA CREAM.)

Chocolate Fig Ice Cream:

Melt 4 ounces chocolate, or carob bar, grated; add ¾ cup turbinado sugar and ½ cup cream. Cook till smooth. Add a pinch of salt, 1 tablespoon vanilla extract, and 1½ cups figs, chopped fine. For special occasions, soak the figs in sherry or wine. Freeze in the refrigerator, stirring occasionally to prevent the figs from clinging together.

Banana Ice Cream:

Add the mashed pulp of bananas in the proportion of 1 banana to each cup of cream. Add a squeeze of lemon juice.

Strawberry Ice Cream:

Add 2 cups crushed strawberries for each 4 cups of cream base. Pour over STRAWBERRY SAUCE.

Strawberry Sauce:

ARROWROOT SAUCE blended with half quantity crushed strawberries, perked up with a little strawberry extract which you can get at most health stores.

And finally, here's the most lucious leftover ever:

Easy Plum Pudding Ice Cream:

Add 1 cup of leftover plum pudding (see PLUM PUDDING and CHRISTMAS PUDDING), baked for a few minutes in the oven (at 200°) so that you can crumble it, to each 4 cups cream base.

Miss Parloa's Lemon Sherbet has a light creamy texture, thanks to the addition of gelatine or carrageen moss.

Lemon Sherbet

Miss Parloa's *New Cook Book*, 1880

"The juice of five lemons, one pint of sugar, one quart of water, one tablespoonful of gelatine [or carrageen moss]. Soak the gelatine in a little of the water. Boil one cupful of the water and dissolve the [soaked] gelatine in it. Mix together the sugar, water, [boiled] gelatine and lemon juice. Turn into the can, and freeze. This is light and creamy."

Makes 2 quarts sherbet.
Note: Use 2 parts ice to one of rock salt when freezing.

❧

Obviously, Hugo Ziemann and Mrs. Gillette, together, have a special touch with ice cream; even their sherbets have a characteristic richness, hard to get in a water ice:

Pineapple Sherbet

Hugo Ziemann and Mrs. Gillette's
White House Cook Book, 1887

"Grate two pineapples and mix with two quarts of water, and a pint [2 cups] of sugar; add the juice of two lemons, and the beaten whites of four eggs. Place in a freezer and freeze."

Makes about 4 quarts sherbet.

❧

Raspberry Sherbet

Mrs. F. L. Gillette and Hugo Ziemann:
The White House Cook Book, 1887

"Two quarts of raspberries (use measuring cup), one cupful of sugar, one pint and a half of water, the juice of a large lemon, one tablespoonful of gelatine. Mash the berries and sugar together and let them stand two hours. Soak the gelatine in cold water to cover. Add one pint of the water to the berries, and strain. Dissolve the gelatine in half a pint of boiling water, add this to the strained mixture and freeze."

For rougher texture, leave unstrained.

And finally, here's a rich and nutritious ice pudding you can make in your refrigerator's freezing tray:

English Ice Pudding

Table Talk, 1901

"Boil ½ cup rice in a pint of water for ½ hour, then drain it and put in a farina [double] boiler with 1 pt. milk. Cook another half hour and pour through a fine sieve (or blend to a cream). Beat the yolks of 6 eggs and one cup of sugar together until light, add them to the rice and milk, cool for a moment, take from the fire and add 1 tablespoonful vanilla ex. [tract] ... Turn this into a freezer and freeze. When frozen stir in lightly 1 pt. whipped cream, cover, pack, and stand aside for 2 hours. ..."

For a more exciting mixture, stir in about ¾ cup of chopped, sun-dried fruits and chopped nuts, mixed. Add just before freezing is reached.

Natural foods ingredients to make 3 quarts ice cream:

½ cup natural brown rice
1 pt (2 c) water
1 pt (2 c) milk
6 yolks of fertilized eggs

1 cup turbinado sugar
1 tbsp real vanilla extract
2 cups heavy cream, whipped

You can add:

dried milk reconstituted in place of fresh;
about ¾ cup mixed, chopped sun-dried fruit and/or nuts.

∾

— 8 —

Cakes and Cookies, Bread and Dropcakes, and Some Oldtime Fritters

A Plum Cake.

TAKE five pounds of fine Flour, and put to it half a pound of Sugar; and of Nutmegs, Cloves, and Mace finely beaten, of each half an ounce, and a little Salt, mix these well together; then take a quart of Cream, let it boil, and take it off, and cut into it three pounds of fresh Butter, let it stand till 'tis melted, and when 'tis blood warm mix with it a quart of Ale-yeast, and a pint of Sack, and twenty Eggs, ten whites well beaten; put six pounds of Currants to your Flour, and make a hole in the middle, and pour in the Milk and other things, and make up your Cake, mixing it well with your Hands; cover it warm, and set it before the fire to rise for half an hour; then put it in the Hoop; if the Oven be hot two hours will bake it; the Oven must be quick; you may perfume it with Ambergrease, or put Sweetmeats in it if you please. Ice it when cold, and paper it up.

An ordinary Cake to eat with Butter.

TAKE two pounds of Flour, and rub into it half a pound of Butter; then put to it some Spice, a little Salt, a quarter and half of Sugar, and half a pound of Raisins stoned, and half a pound of Currants; make these into a Cake, with half a pint of Ale-yeast, and four Eggs, and as much warm Milk as you see convenient; mix it well together, an hour and half will bake it. This Cake is good to eat with Butter for Breakfasts.

Eliza Smith's *The Compleat Housewife*, 1727

Cakes, Cookies—and Oldfashioned Wedding Cake

ALTHOUGH my mother was a fine musician, it was her cake-making that kept us solvent, for there was a firm market in our locale for her teatime tartlets, and other delicious big and little cakes.

Father, on the other hand, was far less active, being a semi-invalid. Nevertheless, all his life he retained that sense of grandeur possessed by South American millionaires, Indian potentates, and imaginative Americans; he took it for granted that tea appeared daily, poured from a fine Georgian teapot when not at the pawnbroker's—its periodic absence annoyed him greatly. We kids served up the cakes on plates of Indian Tree design, which were inherited from my grandmother and bore marks of professional mending in several places. The large cakes were cut with a mother-of-pearl-handled cake knife with a silver blade, not sterling, alas, so unhockable.

Because it's so simple, tea is an inexpensive but charming meal, particularly when the little delicacies are served in the style my father remembered from his childhood. From his armchair he would study the plateful of cakelets with the aloof attitude of the true gourmet. My mother's delicate pastry (which also appeared with touching frequency in the form of *vol au vent*, the French dish that uses leftovers so delectably) made him shake his head in admiration at almost every mouthful.

Artists thrive on the warmth of their audience, and looking back it's no surprise to me that my mother was such a brilliant cook.

Here are some hints for baking that truly great, old-fashioned cake:

Hints on Baking Cake

Don't cut the donkey work by switching on your mixer. When you *mix a cake by hand,* you lift the dough up into the air in a folding movement. This is the secret ingredient of a light-textured cake. A mixer merely mixes, which is why all good cake-makers use the hand method described by Francatelli. (See PLUM CAKE.)

Be sure to let your cake cool off for an hour before removing from the pan. Just set aside someplace.

To *remove the cake from the pan,* ease it out with a heated palette knife inserted between the waxed paper and the side of the pan. Have a mesh tray alongside so that the cake can topple head first onto the safety of the tray. Leave untouched to cool.

If the cake sticks to the pan, hold the obstinate thing upside down over the mesh tray. Beat the hell out of the bottom of the pan with a spoon. The cake will drop down of its own accord. (The same tip holds for little cakes baked in muffin pans.)

Hot cake tends to break, even when handled with great care. So if you're unlucky and your cake fissures apart, seal it with white of egg. Frosting, or other decoration, will hide the patch job.

Always leave your cake to cool on the mesh tray *upside down;* this position keeps the weight to the "rise" of the cake and thus prevents sinking.

A six-pound fruit cake, baked in a slow oven (325°), takes about four hours to cook.

For a table-top smooth surface to a *sandwich or layer cake,* level off the top of the cake; turn the cake upside down so that the dead-smooth bottom of the cake becomes the top. Frost as usual.

Most cakes are baked at low temperature (300° to 325°). However, we used to put little cakes into a hot oven (375°), turning the temperature to low as the cakes were inserted. Thus the heat was briefly at a medium temperature causing the mixture to rise slightly before the actual baking.

A word about using half quantities: if possible, make up the full amount, then divide the mixture in two. Bake in two pans, or half one day and half another, with perhaps a variation in the flavor.

To make up a half quantity: divide the amounts in the recipe in half, except for eggs. Take the half quantity upward, i.e. half of seven eggs equals four, and so forth.

Here are Mrs. Henderson's rules for cake-making, which differ slightly from my mother's method. Incidentally, she too is against halving the ingredients.

Rules for Cake

Mrs. Henderson's *Practical Cooking*, 1876

"Have everything ready before mixing the material—i.e. the ingredients all measured and prepared, and the tins buttered. The sooner the cake is mixed (after the ingredients are ready) and put into the oven, the better. Sift the flour, and have it dry. Mix baking powder or cream of tartar, if used, well into the flour, passing it through the sieve [sifter] several times, if particular. Roll the sugar [necessary only if it's lumpy]; mix sugar and butter together to a cream. The eggs must then be *very, very well* beaten separately. If one person makes the cake, beat the yolks first. If soda is used, dissolve it in the milk, or, if no milk is used, in a little lukewarm water; add it the last thing unless fruit is used, when it should always be rolled in flour, and added the last thing. Cake, to be light, should be baked slowly at first, until the batter is evenly heated all through. Many leave the oven door slightly open for the first ten or fifteen minutes. . . ."

Eliza Smith's Ordinary Cake turned out just great when we baked it—exactly as she directs except for the ale-yeast she uses for rising. (Baking powder was not in her kitchen.) As you may have noticed, her recipe is for a raisin cake, made subtly lighter by the addition of currants.

To make: follow Eliza's instructions *exactly*, sifting in 4 teaspoonfuls of baking powder in place of yeast and using cold milk in place of warm. Use wholegrain, stone-ground flour, regular grind. For spices, add 4 teaspoonfuls mixed spice, or, for a change, 1 table-spoonful real vanilla essence. Put into a hot oven (400°), then bake at moderate (350°) for 1½ hours— as Eliza suggests.

It's a terrific cake, and no trouble to bake.

The cakes that appear over and over in the old cookbooks—seed, plum, orange, pound, almond, and fruit—are favorites still.

Croquante Cake, created by Mrs. Henderson's friend Mrs. Lackland, is almond cake baked in an unusual manner.

The two kinds of almonds usually used are sweet and bitter; the former is the most common and I sug-gest you use it in these recipes—unless of course you get the Jordan, the largest, the most expensive, and the most delicately flavored.

Croquante Cake

Mrs. Henderson's *Practical Cooking*, 1876

"Ingredients: Three-quarters of a pound of shelled almonds, half a pound of citron, three-quarters of a pound of sugar, three-quarters of a pound of flour, and six eggs.

Blanch and halve the almonds, and slice the citron; mix them well together, and roll them in flour; add to them the sugar, then the eggs [well beaten], lastly the flour. Butter shallow pans, and lay in the mixture two inches thick. After it is baked in a quick oven [375°], slice the cake into strips one inch wide, and turn every strip. Return the pan to the oven, and bake the sides a little. When cold, put it away in tin boxes. This cake will keep a year or more, and for reserve use is quite invaluable."

To blanch almonds:

"Put them over the fire in cold water, and let them remain until the water is almost at the boiling point, not allowing them to boil; then throw them into cold water. Remove the skins, and dry the almonds in a cloth before using.

When they are to be pounded for macaroons, *meringues,* etc., they should be first dried for two or three days in a gentle heat."

Miss Shute's cake recipes are more than usually interesting, probably because her book was sponsored by a baking-powder company. If you like, you can take her flavor combinations and add them to your own favorite plain cake mixture.

In each case, follow the general directions above; Miss Shute gives few, so I have rounded her instructions out accordingly.

Seed Cakes

Miss Shute's *American Housewife,*
1879

"Half a cup of butter, a cup and a half of sugar, two eggs, [about] one cup of milk, a teaspoonful of [baking powder], a tablespoonful of caraway seed, a little [ground] ginger, and flour enough to roll out [about 2½ cups]."

Sift the dry ingredients and set aside. Cream the butter and sugar in a mixing bowl to a smooth consistency. Add the sifted flour mixture and the caraway seeds. Drop in the eggs, well beaten. Gradually add the milk and mix until you get a not-too-stiff dough that will sit up nicely in a 3 lb cake tin.

Bake the entire mixture as a cake (at 325°), or drop walnut-sized pieces into muffin tins and bake for about twenty minutes at 375°.

Natural foods ingredients:

½ c butter or margarine
1½ c turbinado sugar
2 fertilized eggs
about 1 c milk
1 tsp baking powder

1 tbsp caraway seeds
a little ground ginger
2½ c wholewheat flour,
pastry grind

❧

I can't think why Rice Cake is not as popular today as it was in Miss Shute's time, for it's a very good cake.

You can bake Rice Cake with rice flour, or with ground rice; the former makes a smooth-textured mixture. The latter takes more trouble (if you do your own grinding), but you'll be rewarded with a cake that's got an interesting, chewy quality.

All rice cakes, by the way, are improved by adding a pinch of salt.

Rice Cake

Miss Shute's *American Housewife,*
1879

"Six ounces of butter, three-quarters of a pound of sugar, seven eggs beaten separately, half a pound of rice flour, half a pound of wheat flour, a teaspoonful of baking powder, and a teaspoonful of lemon extract."

Sift the rice and wheat flour; sift again with the other dry ingredients added. Set aside.

Cream together the sugar and butter, working the mixture to a fine smoothness. Add the flour mixture.

Beat the eggs, the whites and yolks separately, and add, gradually beating them into the mixture.

Natural foods ingredients for a three-pound cake:

6 oz butter or margarine	½ lb wholewheat flour,
¾ lb turbinado sugar	pastry grind
7 fertilized eggs	1 tsp baking powder
½ lb rice flour	1 tsp lemon extract

You can add:

rind of 1 lemon and 1 tsp juice in place of lemon extract;
a little sea salt.

❧

Love Cake

Miss Shute's *American Housewife*, 1879

"Three eggs, five ounces of [turbinado] sugar, six ounces of flour [wholewheat, pastry grind], salt, mace or rose water; to be dropped [on the griddle] and sugar sprinkled on before serving."

An easy-to-fix breakfast for the morning after . . .

❧

A fruit-and-nut cake that's small seems all wrong; actually it's better to bake a large cake because its extra bulk will take a more interesting combination of nuts and fruit. If you lack a large cake tin, divide the mixture and bake in smaller-sized pans.

Hickory Cake

Miss Shute's *American Housewife*, 1879

"One cup of butter, two cups of sugar, four eggs, a cup of sweet milk [or less], four cups of flour, a teaspoonful of baking soda, a little nutmeg, one part [1 cup] of nut meats, half a pint of chopped raisins."

Cream the butter and sugar. Beat the eggs and add to the mixture. Sift the dry ingredients and add, together with 1 cup chopped nut meats and 1 cup chopped raisins. Add enough milk to make a stiffish dough.

Bake for three and a half hours in a 9 x 3½" tin at 320°.

Natural foods ingredients to make a six-pound cake:

1 c butter or margarine
2 c turbinado sugar
4 fertilized eggs
1 c or less fresh milk
4 c wholewheat flour,
    pastry grind

1 tsp baking soda
a little grated nutmeg
1 c chopped nut meats
    (hickory)
1 c chopped raisins
    (stoned)

❧

Berry Cake

Miss Shute's *American Housewife*, 1879

"One cup of sugar, three cups of flour, a piece of butter the size of an egg, three eggs, two cups of [blue] berries, a cupful of sour milk, a teaspoonful of [baking] soda."

Cream the sugar and butter into a smooth paste. Add the eggs, well beaten. Sift the flour and baking soda and add to the mixture. Add two cups of washed and picked-over blueberries. Mix in enough sour milk to make a stiffish dough.

Line a large cake tin with oiled wax paper; bake in a moderate oven (350°) for two hours.

Natural foods ingredients for one large cake:

1 c turbinado sugar
3 c wholewheat flour, pastry grind
2 oz butter or margarine

3 fertilized eggs
2 c blueberries
1 c sour milk
1 tsp baking soda

Cider Cake

Miss Shute's *American Housewife*, 1879

"One cup of butter, two cups of sugar, four eggs, one cup of cider, a teaspoonful of [baking] soda, three cups of flour, a teaspoonful each of cloves, cinnamon and nutmeg, a cup and a half of raisins, a cup and a half of currants, citron."

Beat the butter and sugar to a cream; add each egg separately and beat in to make a smooth paste. Sift the dry ingredients; add to the mixture together with the dried fruit.

Moisten with the cider, using enough to make a stiffish dough. Line a tin with oiled wax paper and bake in a slow oven, 325°, for 2¼ hours.

Natural foods ingredients for one large cake:

1 c butter or margarine	1 tsp each ground
2 c turbinado sugar	cloves, cinnamon,
4 fertilized eggs	and nutmeg
1 c cider or apple juice	1½ c monukka raisins
1 tsp baking soda	1½ c currant and citron
3 c wholewheat flour,	mixed
pastry grind	

❧

More people than you might think bake wedding cake—not a white, towering edifice topped by a tiny tuxedoed guy kissing his bride, but the rich, beautiful plum cake that highlighted wedding festivities centuries ago.

The white wedding cake, with its sickly-sweet icing, belongs to the age of Victorian decoration, and its creation is beyond the capacity of an amateur cook. But the wedding or bride's cake of Eliza Smith's era and later is easy to make, being a rich plum mixture sloshed with a glass or two of brandy.

A couple of years ago, Mick Jagger celebrated his birthday at Madison Square Garden with a gigantic, low-slung one-tiered cake, which was featured in one of the weekly news magazines; you may have seen the photograph. Tiered, or single-plateaued, you can bake a similar-looking cake from either Miss Shute's Wedding Cake or Francatelli's Plum Cake.

Miss Shute heads her chapter on cake-making with this gargantuan number—it weighs over twenty pounds, which gives you an idea of the spreading bounty of nineteenth-century Middle America. (By comparison, Francatelli's Plum Cake weighs in at a mere ten pounds.)

However, whichever recipe you choose to bake for this most wonderful of days, I suggest you tackle the job a couple of weeks before the date. Last-minute jitters could put you off your cake-making form, with not-so-hot results; with two weeks' leeway you'll be free of worry. Store the masterpiece in the refrigerator, or in an airtight tin, until banquet time.

Wedding Cake

Miss Shute's *American Housewife*, 1879

"The materials needed for this cake should be prepared a day or two before the cake is to be made, and put the cake together as early as possible, for it requires the best part of a day to bake it in. It does not need a very hot oven, but a steady heat. It bakes better if made into two or three loaves than in one large one.

"Have the currants picked, washed and dried; the raisins picked, stoned and chopped; the citron cut into small pieces, the flour sifted; the sugar and butter weighted; the eggs broken, the yolks and whites in separate dishes; the spices, brandy, etc. measured; the pan or pans lined with paper, and well-buttered before commencing, so you will not have to leave off after you begin to make the cake.

"Take three pounds of flour, three of sugar, three of butter, three of raisins, six of currants, one of citron, two dozen eggs, one ounce of mace, one of cinnamon, one of nutmeg, half an ounce of cloves, half a pint of brandy.

"To mix it—Stir the butter with your hand to a
cream, then beat the sugar into the butter, add the
yolks of the eggs beaten to a froth. Mix fruit, spice
and flour together; then add them in with beating,
gradually; add the brandy last. Five or six hours
baking will answer for a large loaf."

---

*Natural foods ingredients for a twenty-one pound
cake:*

3 lb wholewheat pastry flour, fine grind	1 lb citron
3 lb turbinado sugar	2 doz fertilized eggs
3 lb sweet butter or margarine	1 oz powdered mace
	1 oz powdered cinnamon
3 lb sun-dried raisins	1 oz grated nutmeg
6 lb currants	½ oz powdered cloves
	½ pt (1 c) brandy

Here are Mr. Francatelli's suggestions for a sump-
tuous cake rich enough for the brides of his era—and
equally good for a simple and joyous wedding today.

He calls the mixture simply:

Plum Cake

Francatelli's *Cook's Guide*, 1888

"Ingredients required: One pound and a half of
flour, one pound and a half of butter, one pound of
fine sugar, one pound of dried cherries (lightly
chopped), one pound and a half of currants, one
pound and a half of candied-orange, lemon, and citron peel—in equal quantities; all these must be cut in
small shreds; eight ounces of ground or pounded
almonds, eight whole eggs, the zest or rind of four
oranges (rubbed on a piece of sugar and afterwards
scraped off), half an ounce of ground spices, consisting of cinnamon, cloves, and nutmeg, mixed in
equal proportions, half a pint of cognac brandy, and
a teaspoonful of salt.

"Place the butter in a large white earthenware pan, and work it with a wooden spoon until it presents the appearance of a creamy substance; next add gradually the flour, sugar, and the eggs, still continuing to work the butter the whole time; when these have been thoroughly mixed, add the cherries, currants, candied peel, ground almonds; brandy, spices and salt must also be added gradually. As soon as these ingredients are incorporated with the butter, let the preparation be poured into a convenient-sized tin (previously lined with double bands of buttered paper), and placed on a stout-made copper baking sheet, with two sheets of buttered paper under the cake, to prevent the composition from becoming calcined by the heat of the oven. A moderate heat will be sufficient to bake the cake, and care must be taken not to put any fire under the oven, so as to increase the heat. These cakes, when baked, should be iced over with sugar. . . ."

Follow Mr. Francatelli's instructions to the letter. Bake your cake at 325° for five hours. Cool for four hours.

As to pans, a circular preserving pan for Miss Shute's cake will hold 20 lbs. of mixture; Mr. Francatelli's ten-pounder will fit a large casserole. If you're completely stuck, check at your local restaurant suppliers—they're sure to have a pan the right size.

Ice over with VANILLA FUDGE FROSTING.

Natural foods ingredients for a ten-pound cake:

1½ lb wholewheat flour, fine pastry grind
1½ lb sweet butter or margarine
1 lb turbinado sugar
1 lb dried cherries (after pitting)
1½ lbs currants
8 oz each candied orange, lemon, and citron peel
8 oz ground almonds
8 fertilized eggs
rind of 4 oranges
½ oz (1 tsp) each powdered cinnamon, ground nutmeg, and ground cloves
½ pt (1 c) brandy
1 tsp sea salt

❧

In England, leftover wedding cake is cut into tiny squares and mailed in decorative white boxes to friends and guests. Tradition has it that if a single girl sleeps with a piece of wedding cake under her pillow, she will dream of her future husband.

Recently, at Sotheby's in London, a piece of Queen Victoria's wedding cake, preserved lovingly for over a century in its tiny box, was auctioned for $70. Was it edible? I don't know—darkened to the color of charcoal, and equally brittle in texture, the once delectable tidbit scarcely invited nibbling.

With its touch of brandy (beloved by Victorian gourmets), Chef Francatelli's Pound Cake makes a good wedding cake mixture; use proportionately as a tier on a plum mixture base, that is, a seven-pound cake (double the quantities given) to ten pounds of Plum Cake.

Pound Cake

Francatelli's Cook's Guide, 1888

"*Ingredients required:* One pound of flour, one pound of butter, one pound of sugar, eight eggs, a wineglass of brandy, a little salt, and the rind of two oranges or lemons rubbed on sugar.

Place the butter in a basin, and work it with a wooden spoon, until it assumes the appearance of thick cream; then add the flour, sugar, and the eggs gradually; when the whole is thoroughly incorporated, add the brandy, sugar, and salt; mix well together, and bake the cakes in any kind of mould (previously spread with butter), or in a tin hoop lined with buttered paper. Plums, currants, almonds, pistachio-kernels, candied-peel, or dried cherries may be added."

Natural foods ingredients for a three-and-one-half pound cake:

1 lb wholewheat flour, pastry, fine grind
1 lb sweet butter or margarine
1 lb turbinado sugar

8 fertilized eggs
¼ c brandy
a little sea salt
rind of 2 oranges or lemons

You can add:

1 c only of: plums, currants, almonds, pistachio-kernels, candied peel, or dried cherries (obtainable at health stores);
or 1 c of a mixture of the above.

How to make a tiered cake:

You won't believe it, but a tiered cake is far easier to create than it looks. Actually, it's two cakes, each baked separately then assembled and glued together with ALMOND PASTE. You can make the base of plum cake, the tier with pound.

When you've baked the cakes and let them cool thoroughly, carefully level them off; then center the pound cake onto the plum cake (the base). Outline the area the former occupies by inserting tooth picks as markers. Remove the pound cake and fill in this area with a layer of ALMOND PASTE ⅓ to ½ inch thick. This filling is thick and sticky and thus has good fixing properties. Place the pound cake back in position; scrape away the excess paste.

Your plum cake should weigh considerably more than the tier, so that it comes out larger than the latter. So before you start making up your mixtures, get some idea of how the proportions of the final result will look by standing the two cake tins one upon the other, as if they were cakes. If you don't like the proportions (the tin representing the pound cake, for instance, may be too small) now is the time to change cake tins—and the amount of cake mixture accordingly.

Some time beforehand, get to know the recipes by baking each cake. This, incidentally, is the golden rule for gaining a reputation as a fine chef—experiment on guests only if you're all in on the cooking.

Allow several days for organizing and baking. When you have decided which mixtures to use, write up a timetable along the following lines:

Make a list of ingredients for the base cake and the tier;

shop for the above;

round up equipment, including outsize baking pans if necessary, making sure your pans will fit in the oven (those stories of the boat-lover who built a super-yacht in his basement, then couldn't engineer it through the door are true);

allow one day for mixing and baking the plum cake;

allow a second day for making the pound cake (the time lag enables the plum cake to "settle");

allow another day for assembling and frosting.

❧

Traditionally, almond paste is used as an under-frosting for a rich, fruit cake, to be covered by regular white icing—or, if you're a conscientious natural-foods cook, by a frosting made with turbinado sugar. (See FUDGE FROSTING.)

Here is Mr. Francatelli's almond paste, created in the traditional manner.

Almond Paste

Francatelli's *Cook's Guide*, 1888

"First, mix eight ounces of very fine pounded almonds, with double that quantity of fine-sifted sugar, a little orange-[flower] water, and sufficient white of eggs to form the whole into a soft paste; spread a coating of this all over the surface of the cake [after it has become cold], and when it is hardened by drying, let the whole be iced over. . . ."

Replacing the "fine-sifted sugar" with turbinado results in a slightly crunchy paste—the concoction is uncooked.

Natural foods ingredients (to cover the top of a ten-pound cake):

8 oz almonds, ground fine in a nut grinder
1 lb turbinado sugar
a little orange-flower water

whites of 5 or 6 fertilized eggs

❧

Vanilla Fudge Frosting

In a double boiler, cook corn syrup, turbinado sugar, and water until gooey. When cool, beat in drops of vanilla essence to taste, until the mixture is the consistency of fudge.

Natural foods ingredients (makes three cups of frosting):

½ c corn syrup   up to ¼ c real vanilla
6 c turbinado sugar   essence
1½ c water

This frosting comes out a pretty beige color. It can also be used as a nut frosting—add 2 to 3 cups of chopped nuts to the above quantity.

Cream Cheese Frosting (White)

This is made of cream cheese, cottage cheese, sugar, white of egg, and sour cream mixed together in the following proportions: ¾ cup cream cheese, ¼ cup cottage cheese, 2 tsp sour cream, and 1 egg white. Put into a bowl, mix and beat thoroughly. Sweeten to taste with honey or sugar. This makes 1¼ cups frosting, which is soft-textured and smooth, unlike a true frosting.

Cover thickly with shredded coconut or chopped walnut meats.

❦

Oldtime cooks tempted their menfolk with cakes and pies rather than cookies. By the time Mrs. Gillette wrote *The White House Cook Book*, however, the American housewife had discovered how quick and easy it is to fill up the cookie jar.

Crisp Cookies

Hugo Ziemann and Mrs. Gillette's
White House Cook Book, 1887

"One cup of butter, two cups of sugar, three eggs well-beaten, a teaspoonful of soda and two of cream tartar, spoonful of milk, one teaspoonful of nutmeg, and one of cinnamon. Flour enough [about 4 cups] to make a soft dough just stiff enough to roll out. Try a pint of sifted flour to begin with, working it in gradually. Spread a little sweet milk over each, and sprinkle with sugar. Bake in a quick oven [400°] a light brown."

Natural foods ingredients to make about seventy-five cookies:

1 c butter or margarine	1 tbsp milk
2 c turbinado sugar	1 tsp nutmeg
3 fertilized eggs, beaten	1 tsp cinnamon
1 tsp soda	(about 4 c) wholewheat
2 tsp cream of tartar	flour pastry grind

You can add:

2 tsp baking powder in place of the soda and cream of tartar.

～

Trifles

Hugo Ziemann and Mrs. Gillette's
White House Cook Book, 1887

"Work one egg and a tablespoonful of sugar to as much flour as will make a stiff paste; roll it as thin as a dollar piece, and cut it into small round or square cakes; drop two or three at a time into the boiling [oil]; when they rise to the surface and turn over they are done; take them out with a skimmer and lay them on an inverted sieve [or paper towel] to drain. When served for dessert or supper, put a spoonful of jelly on each."

∾

A friend of mine, with an eye for the rare and good, collects recipes for hermits, a cookie apparently with a secret past, for it is rarely found except in manuscript books, as those oldtime hand-written recipe books are called in the trade.

It's often impossible to track down the origin of a word, and "hermits" is no exception. However, in France, "hermitage" was a white wine—so perhaps the cookies served with it became "hermits." It's possible, and quite probable. The dictionary, incidentally, is silent on the subject.

A friend of Miss Parloa's, Mrs. L. C. A. (who's too bashful to give her full name) passed along one of these hoarded family recipes for publication. Here it is:

Hermits

Miss Parloa's *New Cook Book,* 1880

"Two cupfuls of sugar, one of butter, one of raisins (stoned and chopped), three eggs, half a teaspoonful of soda, dissolved in three tablespoonfuls of milk; a nutmeg, one teaspoonful each of clove and cinnamon, and six cupfuls of flour. Roll about one-fourth of an inch thick, and cut with a round cake cutter. Bake in a rather quick oven. It will take about twelve minutes."

❧

No cookbook of oldtime recipes would be complete without directions for making Gingersnaps. Mrs. Leach, another of Mrs. Henderson's talented friends, comes up with this richer-than-usual recipe.

Ginger-Snaps

Mrs. Henderson's *Practical Cooking,* 1876

"Ingredients: One pint of molasses, one . . . cupful of brown [turbinado] sugar, one . . . cupful of butter, one tablespoonful of [ground] ginger, and one heaping teaspoonful of [baking] soda dissolved in one tablespoonful of hot water.

"Mix very thick with flour, and roll them very thin."

Thoroughly mix all the ingredients, gradually adding enough wholewheat flour (about 3 cups) to make a stiff dough. Cut into shapes; bake in moderate oven (350°) for ten minutes.

Natural foods ingredients to make about eighty cookies:

2 c molasses
1 c turbinado sugar
1 c butter or margarine
1 tbsp ground ginger

1 tsp baking soda
1 tbsp hot water
about 3 c wholewheat
    flour, pastry grind

❧

Coconut Cookies

Hugo Ziemann and Mrs. Gillette's
White House Cook Book, 1887

"One cup grated coconut, one and one-half cups sugar, three-fourths cup butter, one-half cup milk, two eggs, one large teaspoonful baking-powder, one-half teaspoonful extract of vanilla, and flour enough to roll out."

New York Cookies

Miss Shute's *American Housewife*, 1879

"One cup of butter, one cup of sugar, one egg; a teaspoonful of vanilla, half a teaspoonful of [baking] soda dissolved in a little water; flour enough to roll very soft [about ¾ lb.]. Cut in shapes, and bake in a quick [400°] oven."

Natural foods ingredients:

1 c butter or margarine
1 c turbinado sugar
1 fertilized egg
1 tsp real vanilla extract

½ tsp baking soda
a little water
¾ lb wholewheat flour

Breads and Dropcakes, and Oldtime Fritters

BREAD'S as popular today as it was in the good old days, being savored once more as a delicious and nutritious food; indeed, with some people its status is almost holy, and perhaps they are right. As Miss Shute says:

On Bread-Making and Baking

Miss Shute's *American Housewife*, 1879

"As bread is one of the most essential articles of food, and there is no one thing upon which the health and comfort of a family so much depend, it is of great importance to have good bread well baked. We cannot expect this without care and attention. One must have good flour, good yeast, or baking powder, a good, strong, and willing pair of hands, and a good fire."

Miss Shute's points are well taken, particularly her stress on good ingredients. But just what is good flour? Undoubtedly, wholegrain flour, preferably stone ground, contains the most nutrients, though it's doubtful whether Miss Shute had wholegrain in mind. White flour was well in vogue by the 1870s, though occasionally wholewheat bread appeared on the table, as the accompanying recipe proves.

Entire or Whole Wheat Bread

Emma Telford's *Evening Telegram*
Cook Book, 1908

"Scald a cup of milk; take from the fire and add a
heaping teaspoonful salt, a level teaspoonful sugar
and a tablespoonful shortening. Add a cupful cold
water to the scalded milk and when the mixture is
lukewarm add one-half yeast cake that has been dissolved in one-half cup lukewarm water. Beat in
enough whole wheat flour to make a rather thin
batter, beat well, cover and set aside until light. Then
stir in as much more whole wheat flour as you can
beat in with a spoon. It must be stiff. Beat well, turn
into greased tins, let rise until light, then bake an
hour in a moderate oven."

An excellent whole wheat loaf, unusually light in
texture thanks to the beating. Follow the instructions
to the letter.

Natural foods ingredients:

1 c milk, fresh or dried
reconstituted
1 tsp sea salt
1 tsp turbinado sugar
1 tbsp margarine or
vegetable oil

1 c cold water
1 envelope yeast
dissolved in ½ c
water
1½ to 2 lb whole wheat
flour

❧

This oldtime recipe makes a thicker, chewier loaf.

Bread

Marion Harland and Christine
Herrick's *Modern Cooking*, 1904

"One cake of compressed yeast to every pint of
wetting. *Wetting*—half new milk and half water,
75° to 80° when mixed. Pour enough [lukewarm]
water over the yeast to dissolve it. Mix stiff with [6
to 7 cups sifted] flour, the wetting of milk and water,
and the dissolved yeast. Add, during the kneading, a
level teaspoonful of salt. Knead till perfectly smooth
—it will take at least half an hour. Put in a greased
bread-pan, rub the top over with melted butter, and
keep at a temperature of 75° for three hours, or set
overnight, covering pan with towel; then cover with
lid. In the morning make into loaves and rub over
with melted butter, and put into greased baking tins.
Let the loaves rise for one hour and then bake one
hour. Fine rolls may be made by adding a little butter
and a very little sugar to some of this dough; an
hour and a half before the rolls are wanted the dough
should be rolled out about a quarter of an inch thick,
cut out with a cake-cutter, rubbed over with melted
butter, and folded over. They should be allowed one
hour for rising and should be baked in a quick oven
for twenty minutes."

Don't be surprised, or alarmed, if some cookbook
authors today suggest *two* cakes of yeast to one pint
of water and/or milk. The recipe above is that traditionally used through the ages for baking bread, and
the difference in today's recipes and those of yesteryear is significant.

Within limits, the amount of yeast is dependent
upon the time taken for rising. One cake will "rise"
dough in five hours; two yeast cakes will raise the
same amount of dough within three hours. But pa-

tience and fortitude prevail; you'll be rewarded with a flavorful, full-volumed and well-textured bread by using less yeast.

Pulled Bread

Marion Harland and Christine
Herrick's *Modern Cooking*, 1904

"Take the crust off a newly baked loaf while it is still warm. Pull it (the loaf) lightly and quickly with the fingers of both hands into rough pieces, and bake these in a slow oven until they are lightly browned and crisp."

Buttered Toast

Marion Harland and Christine
Herrick's *Modern Cooking*, 1904

"Toast which is to be buttered should be cut from a loaf one or two days old, in slices about the third of an inch thick. Cut off the crust, and toast the bread before a clear, bright fire. When it is equally and lightly colored on one side turn it to do the other. Place little pieces of butter here and there upon it, put it before the fire for a minute or two till the butter is soft, then spread it upon the toast, taking care not to press heavily upon the bread, or the toast will be heavy. Cut each slice separately into strips an inch and a half broad, and pile these on a hot dish. If one or two slices are cut through together, the butter will sink from the upper piece to the lower. Some cooks hold the toasted bread over a bowl of boiling water for a minute before buttering it. This is to soften it, that it may take the butter more readily. Buttered toast should be prepared at the last moment, and served very hot.

"Dry toast is made as the above with the exception of buttering and steaming."

Rice Waffles

365 Breakfast Dishes, 1901

"Two eggs, ½ a cup boiled rice, 1 ½ cups of flour, 1 teaspoonful baking powder, butter the size of a walnut, a little salt, 1 ¼ cups of milk; mix well and bake at once."

❧

Both rye and oatmeal, which Dr. Lewis extolls, are cereals with protein which can be made complete by adding milk.

Oats come milled two ways: with the seeds intact, and without. The latter, in the form of rolled oats, is of course an inferior product though easier to use.

Both oats and rye are heavily acid, so serve with an alkali fruit such as raisins—a frequent breakfast combination.

You'll really enjoy the good doctor's recipes if you like wholegrain unleavened bread, with its rough toughness and chewy texture; however, his mixture's a little bland, for he makes no mention of salt. So add a pinch of sea salt when you mix the following:

Rye Drop-Cakes

Dr. Dio Lewis's *Our Digestion*, 1872

"Stir rye meal or flour into milk or water [with a pinch of salt], making a batter stiffer than for wheaten cakes. These are a little liable to be heavy; but with a good hot oven, and a little care in handling, they will be light, and furnish an agreeable and wholesome variety to the table."

Oatmeal Cakes

Dr. Dio Lewis's *Our Digestion*, 1872

"Now for one of the most capital articles of food ever eaten. Manage it in this way: Into a quart of cold water, stir oatmeal enough to make it about as thick as hasty pudding (i.e. thick cream). Be sure that the meal is sprinkled on so slowly, and that the stirring is so active, that the mash will have no lumps in it. Now, put it on a tin pan, where it can spread out to half the thickness of a common cracker, and smooth it down with a case-knife. Run a sharp knife across it, so as to divide it into the sized pieces you wish, and then place it in a warm oven and bake slowly, being careful, however, not to brown it. A little butter or suet rubbed over the tin pan before spreading the mush, will prevent sticking. When it is done, eat as you would bread. You have one of the most delicious articles of food ever eaten; besides, it will keep for some time. These oatmeal cakes constitute an admirable food, delicious and nutritious."

Agreed, Dr. Lewis—but you forget that pinch of salt again.

Eliza Leslie's little tome, *The Indian Meal Book*, traveled across the Atlantic in the opposite direction from that taken by most cookbooks—for a reason historically important. During the 1840s, Europe suffered a failure of the potato crop, which affected the British Isles and Ireland, the latter disastrously.

To alleviate the "sufferings of the poor," Indian meal was imported together with Eliza Leslie's cookbook. Eliza's British publishers felt that because she'd lived in England, of all American cooks she'd best understand the problems of the British people, who'd therefore find her recipes easy to follow. Actually, Eliza's corn recipes are so simple a moron could make them with no trouble.

Nantucket Pudding is one of the more sophisticated corn dishes Eliza sent over to her English cousins.

Nantucket Pudding

Eliza Leslie's *Indian Meal Book*, 1846

6 large ears of young soft Indian corn
A quarter of a pound of fresh butter
A quarter of a pound of sugar
1 pint of milk
Four eggs
A nutmeg, and three or four blades of mace, powdered

"Having first boiled the corn for a quarter of an hour, take a large grater and grate the grains down from the cob. Then add the butter (cut into little bits) and the sugar, gradually. Having stirred them well into the corn, then the mixture with the milk, add the spice. Beat the eggs very light and then stir them gradually into the other ingredients. Butter a deep white dish. Put in the pudding, set it directly into a hot oven, and bake it two hours. Send it to table warm, and eat it with sweetened cream, or with butter and sugar.

"It is not good cold; but what is left, may be used in a cloth next day and boiled half an hour. It will then be a good boiled pudding."

❧

Fritters were popular with nineteenth-century cooks both as breakfast dishes and desserts. In fact, both Mrs. Henderson and Miss Parloa devote several pages to this delicious and useful dish. For fritters are quickly cooked, especially if the batter is made beforehand.

Mrs. Henderson gives a batter taken from *The French Cook,* which she calls:

French Fritter Batter

Mrs. Henderson's *Practical Cooking,*
1876

"Put a heaping cupful of flour into a bowl; add two yolks of eggs, a table-spoonful of olive oil, which is better than melted butter, and one or two table-spoonfuls of brandy, wine, or lemon-juice. Stir it well, adding, little by little, water enough to give it the thickness of ordinary batter. This may be used at once; but it is better to put it away for a day, or even for a week. At the moment of cooking, stir in well the whites of two eggs beaten to a very stiff froth.

"The brandy, wine, or lemon-juice may be omitted if preferred."

Natural foods ingredients:

1 heaping c wholewheat flour, pastry grind
2 fertilized eggs
1 tbsp olive oil

1 or 2 tbsp brandy, wine, *or* lemon juice (optional)
water

You can add:

a few grains sea salt.

Pineapple, Apple Preserves, or Peach Fritters

Mrs. Henderson's *Practical Cooking*, 1876

"Add a pint or less of any of these fruits, cut into small pieces, to . . . the above receipt. When done, sprinkle sugar over the tops."

-Miss Parloa suggests adding sugar to the batter mixture when making fruit fritters.

❧

Apple Fritters

Miss Parloa's *New Cook Book*, 1880

"Pare and core the apples, and cut in slices about one-third of an inch thick. Dip in the batter, and fry six minutes in boiling fat. Serve on a hot dish. The apples may be sprinkled with sugar and a little nutmeg, and let stand an hour before being fried. In that case, sprinkle them with sugar when you serve them."

Don't pare the apples, and serve with honey in place of sugar.

❧

Clam Fritters

Miss Parloa's *New Cook Book*, 1880

"Drain and chop a pint of clams, and season with salt and pepper. Make a fritter batter as directed, using, however a *heaping* pint of flour, as the liquor in the clams thins the batter. Stir the clams into this, and fry in boiling fat."

If you're using Mrs. Henderson's batter, above, add 1 level tablespoon extra flour to her heaping cupful.

Chicken Fritters

Miss Parloa's *New Cook Book*, 1880

"Cut cold roasted or boiled chicken or fowl in small pieces, and place in an earthen dish. Season well with salt, pepper and the juice of a fresh lemon. Let the meat stand one hour; then make a fritter batter, and stir the pieces into it. Drop, by the spoonful, into boiling fat, and fry till a light brown. Drain, and serve immediately. Any kind of cold meat, if tender, can be used in this way."

❧

9

Curry Powders, Potted Spreads, and Other Oddments; Wines and a Potpourri of Beauty Nostrums

To make Apricock Wine.

TAKE three pounds of Sugar, and three quarts of Water, let them boil together and scum it well; then put in six pounds of Apricocks pared and stoned, and let them boil till they are tender; then take them up, and when the Liquor is cold bottle it up. You may, if you please, after you have taken out the Apricocks, let the Liquor have one boil with a sprig of flower'd Clary in it; the Apricocks make Marmalade, and is very good for present spending.

To promote Breeding.

LET the Party take of the Syrup of stinking Orace a spoonful night and morning, for a week or more; then as follows: Take 3 pints of good Ale, boil in it the Piths of three Ox-Backs, half a handful of Clary, a handful of Nep (or Cat Bos,) a quarter of a pound of Dates stoned, sliced, and the Pith taken out; a handful of Raisins of the Sun stoned, 3 whole Nutmegs prick'd full of holes. Boil all these till half be wasted; strain it out, and drink a small Wine-glass full at your going to Bed. As long as it last accompany not with your Husband. During the taking, or some time before, be very chearful, and let nothing disquiet you.

Take Shepherd's-purse a good handful, and boil it in a pint of Milk till half be consumed, and drink it off.

Eliza Smith's *The Compleat Housewife*, 1727

Oldtime housewife-cooks give us a unique picture of their homes, and of an era. They zealously passed along with their treasured recipes such household hints as cleaning plaster casts (with a feather duster) and making paste for scrap books (mix a brew of flour, alum, cloves and sassafras)—together with recipes for perfume and curry powder, preserves and wines, all packed higgledy-piggledy into the last pages of their recipe books.

There's much good stuff amongst these helpful hints. What housewife today, for instance, needs pressuring to follow Lafcadio Hearn's advice on cleaning house: "House cleaning should commence at the top of the house and work downwards. In this case, it may be undertaken *by spells, with intervening rests.*" The italics are mine, inserted as I wilt over my broomhead.

Then, too, I have cider brewing in my kitchen, the recipe taken directly from Eliza Smith. (Get a quart bottle of *un*pasteurized apple juice, obtainable from health stores during the fall; open up and take off a glassful. Throw in a few raisins, ½ cup turbinado sugar and leave until fermenting microcosms stop chugging, about two to three weeks. Skim, decant—and fill up the glasses.)

On the other hand, I passed up Eliza's well-meaning directions on making a "Necklace for Children Cutting Teeth"—with other herbs, she strings henbane, a powerful but poisonous aphrodisiac guaranteed to quieten any fractious child—perhaps forever. A pathetic comment on those good old days.

But the unwittingly murderous Eliza comes back to my heart with her recipe for Apricock Wine (above). I, too, find her economical idea of using pulp from juiced apricots (and other fruits and vegetables) "very good for present spending."

One of the most useful recipes I unearthed is this seasoning powder. You can put it into sauces, sprinkle it over vegetables and fish; it's great with scrambled eggs. In fact, a pinch will pep up any savory dish you can think of.

Aromatic Herbaceous Seasoning

Francatelli's *Cook's Guide*, 1888

"Take of nutmegs and mace one ounce each, of cloves and peppercorns two ounces of each, one ounce of dried bay-leaves, three ounces of basil, the same of marjoram, two ounces of winter savory, and three ounces of thyme, half an ounce of cayenne-pepper, the same of grated lemon-peel, and two cloves of garlic; all these ingredients must be well pulverized in a mortar, and sifted through a fine wire sieve, and put away in dry corked bottles for use."

A piece of nylon curtain net makes a good substitute for a fine wire sieve. Have someone stretch it tightly and hold in place over a bowl. Press the seasoning through with a wooden spoon, as you would through a sieve.

Natural foods ingredients to make a little over one pound seasoning:

1 oz ground nutmegs	3 oz marjoram
1 oz ground mace	2 oz savory
2 oz ground cloves	3 oz thyme
2 oz peppercorns	½ oz cayenne pepper
1 oz dried bay leaves	½ oz grated lemon peel
3 oz basil	2 cloves garlic

❧

If you cook Indian or Far East food, you're probably on the lookout for good chutney and curry-powder recipes.

This chutney is easy to make—it depends mostly on your pounding ability—and sufficiently "Indian" to rate a top place on your spice shelf.

Indian Chutney

Marion Harland and Christine
Herrich's *Modern Cooking*, 1904

"Boil together a pint of good vinegar with half a pound of [tart cooking] apples, peeled, cored, and quartered. When pulped and cool, add, first pounding them separately in a mortar and afterwards together, the following ingredients: 4 ounces of stoned raisins, 8 ounces of brown sugar, 2 ounces of garlic, and 2 ounces of mustard seed; mix these well with 2 ounces of powdered ginger, the same of salt, and 1 ounce of cayenne. Put the mixture into an earthenware jar, and set the jar in a warm corner by the fire until next morning, when the chutney may be put into small jars and (the paper or plastic covers) tied down. It will keep good a year or two. Time to stew apples, until soft."

Put the concoction near a radiator, or better still, on your yogurt maker, if its base is broad enough.

Quickie Version: Boil the apples and vinegar as directed; put with all other ingredients into the blender and whirl away.

Natural foods ingredients to make two pounds plus of chutney:

1 pt cider vinegar	2 oz mustard seed
½ lb tart cooking apples	2 oz powdered ginger
4 oz monukka raisins	2 oz sea salt
1 c turbinado sugar	1 oz cayenne
2 oz garlic	

❧

Curry Powder—A Genuine Indian Receipt

Miss Shute's *American Housewife*,
1879

"Turmeric, coriander, black pepper, four ounces each; fenugreek, three ounces; ginger, two ounces; cummin seed, ground rice, one ounce each; Cayenne pepper, cardamon, half an ounce each. Pound, sift and bottle."

Makes 20 ounces.

Curry Powder—American

Miss Shute's *American Housewife*,
1879

"One ounce of ginger, one ounce of coriander seed, two ounces of turmeric, and half an ounce of Cayenne pepper; pound, sift and bottle it."

Makes 4½ ounces.

One of the joys of an English breakfast is potted fish spread on crunchy chunks of wholewheat toast. My favorites are bloater and shrimp.

Potting

Mrs. Henderson's *Practical Cooking*,
1876

"In England, potting is an everyday affair for the cook. If there be ham, game, tongue, beef, or fish on the table one day, you are quite sure to see it potted on the next day at lunch or breakfast. It is a very good way of managing left-over food, instead of invariably making it into hashes, stews etc. These potted meats will keep a long time. They are not good unless thoroughly pounded, reduced to the smoothest possible paste, and free from any unbroken fibre."

Potted Fish

Mrs. Henderson's *Practical Cooking,*
1876

"Cut out the pieces of fish; season with pepper, salt, and cloves if you like; then put them into a dish; cover closely. . . . Bake one hour. When cold, press them into the pot, and cover well with butter, etc."

Potted Bloaters

Francatelli's *Cook's Guide,* 1888

"Cut off the heads and tails from six fresh-cured Yarmouth-bloaters; immerse them in scalding water, to remove the skins; take out the backbones, and put them in a stewpan with six ounces of clarified butter, a bit of mace, a teaspoonful of anchovy, and a pinch of cayenne; simmer all together over a slow fire for ten minutes; pound in a mortar, rub through a coarse hair sieve, and use this preparation to fill small pots, which must be covered in with clarified butter, and kept in a cool place for use.

"*Note:* Smoked salmon or dried haddocks, treated in the same manner as bloaters, will furnish other delicate relishes for the breakfast and tea table."

Try out first with two bloaters, or ½ lb fish and 2 oz butter and ¼" anchovy paste in tube.

❧

And for total vegetarians, Marion Harland and Christine Terhune Herrick suggest this nutritious Nut Butter:

Nut Butter

Marion Harland and Christine
Herrick's *Modern Cooking*, 1904

"Shell the nuts, using only the nut-meat. Purchase a stone mortar and pestle, such as are used by the apothecary. (They will be found to answer for many other purposes.) Pound and grind the nuts with the pestle until they have become a cream. If of too thick a consistency, add a little water; then put into corked glass jars. In summer nut-butter is apt to become rancid, so I would not advise the making of too large quantities. The Brazil nuts are frequently added in part to the other nuts, being made into butter so as to enhance the flavor. Almond, Brazil, pecans, walnuts, and peanuts make the best butter.

"When using almonds always remove the brown skin by steeping in hot water for a few minutes, then rub off with a coarse towel."

Ms. Harland's point about adding Brazil nuts is worth noting. These nuts are rich in calcium and phosphorus, and incomplete in protein; consequently, they should be eaten sparingly and chewed well. A butter made of Brazil nuts only is overly rich.

❧

Orange Butter

Mrs. Rundell's *Domestic Management*,
1806

"Boil six eggs hard, beat them in a mortar with two ounces of fine [turbinado] sugar, three ounces of butter, and two ounces of blanched almonds beaten to a paste. Moisten with orange-flower water, and when all is mixed, rub it through a colander on a dish, and serve [on] sweet biscuits. . . ."

Worth all the beating and pounding—but some blenders will do the job.

Jams and jellies are "jelled" by the pectin in the fruit. You'll be glad to know that strawberries are high in pectin, consequently trouble-free when preserved.

Miss Shute's recipe is one used by cooks the world over and is easy to remember: one pound of sugar to one pound of strawberries (after picking over).

Strawberry Jam

Miss Shute's *American Housewife*,
1879

"Mash the berries with a wooden spoon; put them into the preserving kettle, and let them cook ten minutes; then add the sugar, allowing a pound and a half of sugar to each quart of raw berries, or a pound of sugar to each pint after it is stewed."

Don't mash all the berries; leave a number whole for so-called "whole" strawberry jam.

To stop the strawberries from sticking to the pan while stewing, add a quarter cup water, but no more or the jam will not jell.

Jam is ready to pot when a tablespoonful, dropped onto a saucer, jells to the right consistency (about 45 minutes).

❧

Grape Jelly

Miss Shute's *American Housewife,*
1879

"Strip from their stalks some fine ripe grapes, and stir them with a wooden spoon over a gentle fire until all have burst and the juice flows freely from them. Strain it off through a jelly [cheese] cloth or bag. Measure, and to each pint of juice allow fourteen ounces of sugar. Put the juice on to boil for twenty minutes; then stir in the sugar and boil fifteen minutes longer, keeping it constantly stirred and well skimmed."

Very easy to make; seal in airtight jars when cool enough to pour in without cracking the jar. (Put a spoon in and pour the jelly onto it—the metal takes off the heat.)

For even easier fixing, put the grapes into a juice extractor instead of cooking first and straining through a cloth. Then carry on with the rest of the recipe.

Natural foods ingredients to make two pounds jelly:

2 to 3 lb grapes to make   14 oz turbinado sugar
  1 pt juice

❧

Making wine at home is fraught with unpredictables, but easy enough once you know the lore. So before attempting these recipes, I suggest you consult a good book on wine-making, such as *Amateur Wine Making* by S. M. Tritton (Dover, 1955).

Like bathtub gin, homemade wine can be heady stuff. The most potent I've tasted is the homemade cider or perry (cider made with pears) brewed by the not-so-simple cottagers living in England's West Country. Quaffed by the wayside on a hot summer's day, one glass can slice the legs from under you.

Currant Wine

Miss Shute's *American Housewife*, 1879

"To four quarts of currants put five pounds of sugar, and half a gallon of water. Mash and squeeze the currants and let it stand until February or March, then bottle."

Raspberry Wine

Peterson's Magazine, 1858

"Take three pounds of raisins, wash clean and stone them thoroughly; boil two gallons of spring water for half an hour; as soon as it is taken off the fire pour it into a deep stone jar, and put in the raisins, with six quarts of raspberries and two pounds of [turbinado] sugar; stir it well together, and cover it closely, and set it in a cool place; stir it twice a day; then pass it through a sieve; put the liquor into a closed vessel, adding one pound more loaf sugar; let it stand for a day and a night to settle, after which bottle it, adding a little more sugar."

Wines from the *fin de siècle* cellars of Delmonico's —what misty figures float in their bouquet: round-hipped ladies drenched in jewels, hair pompadoured and cheeks discreetly rice-powdered, and escorted by famous gallants like the eccentric James Gordon Bennett, publisher of the old *New York Herald*.

Delmonico's: the lilting name christens a restaurant whose fine cuisine symbolized an age, and which was the mecca of the fashionably prominent from both sides of the Atlantic. Lillian Russell displayed her plush beauty against its decor, while Colonel Mann watched eagle-eyed for tidbits to chronicle in his *Town Topics*—a notorious magazine read by the erring great with panic. Sexual disgrace in this tight-laced era heralded bankruptcy, both social and financial.

And all the while, as the celebrities chatted and gossiped under the winking sparkle of the chandeliers, the great chef, Filippini, served his Terrapin à la Baltimore, and his Sweetbreads Braised (appropriately) à la Financière, and from a topaz sea in a silver bowl, poured into delicate crystal glasses his famous Champagne Cup—also immortalized in many mythical slippers.

Champagne Cup

Filippini's *The Table*, 1889

"Squeeze the juice of half a good-sized, sound lemon into a fancy glass pitcher large enough to contain five pints; sweeten with one tablespoonful of powdered sugar, then add two ponies of red curacoa, one bottle of plain soda, and two slices of cucumber-rind. Pour in three pints of any brand of champagne, adding about a quarter of a pound of ice, then mix thoroughly with a spoon, and ornament the punch nicely with strawberries, very thin slices of pineapple, a finely sliced, medium-sized orange, and half a bunch of fine, fresh mint; send the cup to the table with six champagne-glasses."

For those who enjoy spicy drinks—here's a humdinger:

Vegetarian Coffee

Marion Harland and Christine
Herrick's *Modern Cooking*, 1904

"One teaspoonful each of whole allspice, cinnamon, cloves, crushed nutmeg, blade of mace, quarter of bay leaf; steep in 1 quart of water half an hour; strain in hot pot, adding 1 lump of sugar [or honey to taste] for each guest. A pitcher of hot cream is at hand for the hostess to 'dress' the coffee before the latter is passed. Rose-disks are dropped into the beverage."

For rose disks, read petals—a charming idea. And a pitcher of hot milk, of course, can act for cream.

If this candy recipe dates to the time of Lafcadio's grandfather, then it surely was chewed by the Founding Fathers themselves.

Molasses Candy of Our Grandfathers' Time

Lafcadio Hearn's *La Cuisine Créole*,
1885

"One quart of molasses, and butter the size of an egg. Stew over a brisk fire till it will harden on being dropped into cold water. A teaspoonful of essence of wintergreen should be added when it is almost done. Pull it while warm, with buttered hands, and cut in sticks."

Here's a nifty little candy recipe (Lafcadio's, of course) which uses egg whites, leftover or otherwise. Pass around with a glass of your best homemade wine.

Chocolate Kisses

Lafcadio Hearn's *La Cuisine Créole*,
1885

"One-half pound of [turbinado] sugar, one ounce of finely-powdered chocolate. Mix the sugar and chocolate together, and then mix it with the whites of four eggs well beaten. Drop on buttered paper and bake."

You can make this with carob in place of chocolate; in that case, use a little more.

No housewife in this era of ornamentation would serve pudding or cake undecorated.

Her medium for this culinary pop art was candied fruit and peel, which is great fun to use, and worth the bother of preparation.

To Candy Fruit

Lafcadio Hearn's *La Cuisine Créole*,
1885

"After peaches, quinces, plums, or citron, have been preserved, take them from the syrup, and drain them on a sieve. To a pound of . . . sugar, put a small cup of water, and when it is dissolved, set it over a moderate fire, and let it boil; when it boils, put in the fruit to be candied, and stir continually until the sugar granulates over the fruit; then take it up, and dry it in a warm oven. If not sufficiently candied, repeat the operation."

White sugar will give a light glaze, as opposed to turbinado, which gives a slightly honeyed look. You take your choice.

Candied Pumpkin

Lafcadio Hearn's *La Cuisine Créole,*
1885

"Peel a piece of pumpkin, and cut it in thin slices. Make a nice, thick syrup of brown [turbinado] sugar and water, and put the pumpkin into it, with a little of the juice of the lemon. Boil this until the pumpkin is nicely candied. Mace, or other spices, [e.g., nutmeg] may be used for flavoring instead of lemon, if preferred. It may be eaten hot with meats at dinner, and is equally nice, when cold, for supper or lunch."

Brown sugar is white sugar colored with molasses. So when using turbinado, mix in a little molasses.

Natural foods ingredients:

Pieces of pumpkin, cut in thin slices
turbinado sugar
molasses in the proportion of 1 tbsp to 1 c sugar

lemon juice *or* powdered mace *and/or* grated nutmeg

❧

If by now you're tired of fancy food and yearn for the simple life of yesteryear, I suggest you read Mrs. Rundell's good advice, but with a not-too-cynical eye; the picture she conjures up of life for the poor in early nineteenth-century England is not a pretty one. Of her smug hypocrisy, let's just say she, too, was a victim of her era. By other counts, she seems to have been a charming lady, if no Florence Nightingale.

Cookery for the Poor
General Remarks and Hints

Mrs. Rundell's *Domestic Management*, 1806

"I promised a few hints, to enable every family to assist the poor of their neighborhood at a very trivial expense; and these may be varied or amended at the discretion of the mistress.

"Where cows are kept, a jug of skimmed milk is a valuable present, and a very common one.

"When the oven is hot a large pudding may be baked and given to a sick or young family; and thus made the trouble is little: Into a deep coarse pan put a half pound of rice, four ounces of coarse sugar or treacle, two quarts of milk and two ounces of dripping; set it cold into the oven. It will take a good while, but be an excellent solid food.

"A very good meal may be bestowed in a thing called brewis, which is thus made: Cut a very thick upper crust of bread, and put it into the pot where salt-beef is boiling and nearly ready; it will attract some of the fat, and when swelled out will be no unpalatable dish to those who rarely taste meat."

Occasionally as a child, I'd go with my mother to visit an ancient friend, and as I write I can still sense the mysterious fragrance that spread cloudlike around her bowl of potpourri. I always made noisy sniffs at the faded petals.

The efficient, hard-working Miss Shute becomes herself as she talks lovingly of her potpourri bowl; and like her flowers and herbs, her personality emerges simple, feminine, and very Victorian.

Perfume for Jars
Pot-Pourri

Miss Shute's *American Housewife,*
1879

"Take, for the foundation, rose leaves and salt prepared during the rose season, turning and mixing the mass and adding constantly to it for two months. Then place a portion of it on the bottom of the jar, spread a layer of raw cotton over, sprinkled with powdered cloves, mace, nutmeg, allspice, cinnamon, orris root, carraway and fennel seeds (bruised), cardamom pods and seeds, or sprays of lavender, a handful of sage, thyme and rosemary, shavings of cedar, any highly perfumed flowers, leaves of rose and lemon geraniums, a sprinkling of camphor, sprigs of peppermint, spearmint and a little musk. Any odoriferous material, indeed, will add piquancy to the pot-pourri. I sprinkle the layers with very strong vinegar, and add a handful of salt each week during the time of putting in fresh materials. Cologne, essential oils of various kinds, and the sachet odors sold at a comparatively low price in the wholesale drug stores prove fine additions. Such jars opened daily for fifteen minutes fill a house with odors as spicy and delicious as those wafted from the realms of 'Araby the blest.' "

❧

Scent Powder

Miss Shute's *American Housewife*,
1879

"Coriander, orris root, rose leaves and aromatic calamus, each one ounce; lavender flower, ten ounces; rhodium, one-fourth of a drachm; mush, five grains. These are to be mixed and reduced to a coarse powder. This scents clothes as if fragrant flowers had been pressed in their folds."

Lavender Scent Bag

Miss Shute's *American Housewife*,
1879

"Take of lavender flowers free from stalks, half a pound; dried thyme and mint, of each half an ounce; ground cloves and carraway, of each a quarter of an ounce; common salt, dried, one ounce; mix the whole well together, and put into silk or cambric bags. In this way it will perfume the drawers and linens very nicely."

Husband-hunting? Mrs. Gillette has irresistible bait.

Odoriferous or Sweet-Scenting Bags

Hugo Ziemann and Mrs. Gillette's
White House Cook Book, 1887

"Lavender flowers, one ounce; pulverized orris, two drachms; bruised rosemary leaves, half ounce; musk, five grains; attar of rose, five drops. Mix well, sew up in small flat muslin bags, and cover them with fancy silk or satin.

"These are very nice to keep in your bureau drawer or trunk, as the perfume penetrates through the contents of the trunk or drawers. An acceptable present for a single gentleman."

∾

To Make the Complexion Soft and Fine

Miss Shute's *American Housewife*, 1879

"Make a linen bag large enough to hold a quart of bran, put it in a vessel and pour two quarts of boiling water on it; let it stand all day, and at night on going to bed, take the bag out, and wash the face with the bran water; in the morning wash it off entirely with distilled rain water. In a very short time it will make a coarse skin feel like velvet."

∾

Centuries after their demise Cleopatra and the beautiful Greek *hetaira* Phrygne, as well as Madame DuBarry still reign as queens of beauty today. So too, from a later age, does Sarah Bernhardt.

Bernhardt was the theatrical goddess for whom Oscar Wilde reportedly wrote his notorious *Salome*, a hit played by every stock company that could muster up seven diaphanous veils and a plump beauty to discard them.

The Divine Sarah's cosmetic recipes were a secret guarded both by the great actress and Dr. Caissarato, her physician and beauty culturist. In a unique dual interview, held when Bernhardt was in her sixties, she and the renowned doctor parted with the secrets of the homemade beautifiers to an enterprising newshen.

When asked what beauty regimen he recommended, the doctor replied: "What I make Madame Bernhardt do—diet, exercise, bathe."

Plus ça change: In Bernhardt's day the ideal weight for a woman 5'6" tall was 142 pounds, and even with that criterion I'm sorry to report the fascinating Sarah spread too widely.

Bernhardt's Wrinkle Eradicator

"Alum 60 grains. Almond milk, 1 ½ ounces. Rosewater, 6 ounces. Dissolve the alum in the rose-water, then pour slowly into the almond milk, stirring constantly. Bottle and use when needed."

And refrigerate.

The secret ingredient Bernhardt left out: egg whites.

Cleopatra reportedly bathed in asses' milk. The more practical Dr. Caissarato recommends this mixture of herbs as a "good substitute for the celebrated beauty bath of milk—the one Sarah Bernhardt has used successfully for years":

Bernhardt's Beauty Bath

"Marshmallow flowers, half a pound; hyssop herb, one quarter of a pound; bran flour, four pounds."

Toss a handful into the tub and luxuriate. Tone up the skin with a splash of cold water.

Bernhardt's Tonic Vinegar

"Oil of bergamot, 12 grammes; oil of citron, 10 grammes; tincture of benzoin, 12 grammes; extract of lavender, 30 grammes; pure white vinegar, 1¾ pints. "Let infuse for ten days, then bottle for use."

This lotion can be used with great effect on the face and neck—according to Bernhardt.

Are these oldtime concoctions safe to use? Many of Bernhardt's ingredients appear in beauty recipes created by Alexandra York, who authored *The Natural Skin Care and Beauty Cook Book* (Ballantine, 1973) —which proves there's little new in this old world.

As I opened my newest antique-book purchase, the 1858 volume of *Peterson's Magazine*, a delicate mauve bloom, faded by over a century of dead life, floated to the floor.

As I replaced it I wondered whose was the hand that pressed these age-old flowers between the leaves of the old volume.

Incidentally, the more famous *Godey's Ladies' Book* features no such feminine handicrafts, while *Graham's Magazine* ran works by authors like Edgar Allan Poe —at least in its early issues.

But *Peterson's* gets to the feminine heart; alongside the sugar-sweet poems appear receipts for making bonnets and tulle undersleeves, gooseberry jam ("to every six pounds of fruit add a quart of cold spring water. . . .")—and pressed flowers.

To Dry Plants

Peterson's Magazine, 1858

"Be careful to gather the specimens in dry weather, after the dew has evaporated. The best way to take them home is in the crown of a hat, or a tin sandwich box. Then taking up each specimen singly, lay it smooth between two sheets of blotting-paper, and then place it inside a large book; then another specimen a few leaves distant, and so on, till the book is full. This done, tie it up tightly with a string, and place two flat irons on it. Thus the plants are to remain for a day, and then be changed into fresh blotting paper, to dry them still more, and so on for four or five days, when they will all be found a good color, and fit to put away. . . ."

If you like shortcuts, the editor gives this advice:
When the plant is ready to be dried within the sheets of blotting paper

". . . iron it with a large smooth heater [your electric iron] strongly warmed, till all the moisture is dissipated. Some plants require more moderate heat than others, and herein consists the nicety of the experiment; but we have generally found that if the iron be not too hot, and is passed rapidly, yet carefully over the surface of the blotting paper, it answers the purpose equally well with plants of almost every variety of hue and thickness."

❧

"God gave food, but man made cooks." (Miss T. S. Shute, in the foreword to *The American Housewife,* 1879)

Useful Information

Oldtime Hints for Saving Fuel—and *Dollars*

The oldtime housewife kept a wary eye on domestic bills; the pennies she saved here and there made big savings in her enormous household accounts.

Here's a list of hints to help you conserve both fuel and dollars, some practised by those redoubtable ladies of the good old days.

To stew a delicious casserole, slowly and lovingly, set up a haybox, or its modern equivalent made with plastic shavings, shredded newspapers or even a warm blanket.

The haybox was used extensively by oldtime English housewives. Its construction is primitively simple, consisting of a box filled with hay (or nylon filler, etc.), into which you embed a casserole of beans, or whatever, previously brought to the boil. On the principle of the thermos, the original heat is conserved by the insulating material so that the casserole cooks gently over a period of several hours. Foods cooked this way are simply delicious, and cost only the fuel used in bringing the casserole to the boil.

Don't turn on your oven, willy-nilly, to cook one dish only, or to brown already cooked food; you can slip the latter under the broiler. When you do use your oven, take a tip from the oldtime housewife with her wood-burning range: fill up all shelves and corners. If you're roasting chicken or turkey, for instance, bake potatoes alongside, and pop in a turnip for a change. If you're baking a pie, include a custard, which can be served cold later.

The rule for filling up your oven, however, is dictated, not by the space available as you might think, but by the temperature at which the different dishes are cooked, and by their aroma, which may permeate. Thus a delicately sweet custard should not be cooked with a sniff-watering turkey (a savory could) but alongside a covered casserole of beans, for instance. Then, too, you obviously cannot bake cookies which need a quick spurt of high temperature with that same bean casserole, which needs the gentlest heat. Nor can you bake a pie for forty-five minutes, then yank it from the oven while a cake is in the process of baking. Opening the door—with the consequent blast of cool air—will surely un-rise the latter.

Lastly, on a baking or long-cooking day, save fuel by making the kitchen your center for socializing. It's a great place, anyway.

Steaming has come back into style, and here again oldtime cooks can pass on a hint or two. Don't waste the water boiling in the bottom of the steamer—use it for cooking potatoes or other root vegetables: don't steam one, but two puddings, set one atop the other.

Potatoes nestled in the warmth of embers cook as though kissed by the gods, while the same warmth will set the yogurt bacillus working.

Think of leftovers as garnish or salad. For the former, drop little blobs around, say, a dish of rice. For the latter serve as is dunked in mayonnaise.

The problem of stale bread was neatly solved by the oldtime housewife. She baked it in the oven then crushed it in a machine like a meat chopper, made for the purpose; you can crumble yours down with a rolling pin just as easily. These baked crumbs are delicious sprinkled over fried foods, or as is over cooked vegetables, or salad. Then, too, you can use recipes featuring stale bread, such as BROWN BREAD ICE CREAM or HALF HOUR PUDDING. Or you can bake your leftover bread as rusks—truly delicious, especially spread with nut butter.

Many oldtime recipes use egg yolks only, leaving you stranded with extra whites.

Actually, the yolk is far more nutritive than the

white, containing protein, fat, and lecithin, which has a high phosphorus content. Also present in yolks are rich supplies of iron, potassium, calcium and sulphur, and vitamins A and D, but little vitamin B. Both yolks and whites are acid-forming.

What to do with extra egg whites? Meringue is the obvious answer, except the number of lemon meringue pies you'd want to bake is surely limited. One solution is to use extra egg white as a fortifier, particularly in milk, which it turns into a frothy delight in the blender. Then, too, there's the family dog or cat who'll relish a little egg white stirred into his (or her) dinner.

Extra egg white can be used to lighten cake and bread mixture, and to froth up omelets and scrambled eggs.

Or take the organized way out: schedule yolk-only with egg-white recipes listed in Appendix B.

No natural-foods housewife worthy of the title throws away the nutritious pulp rejected from a juicing job. Like Eliza Smith, in her recipe for Apricock Wine, she uses the leftover glop in puddings, breads (carrot, for instance), or to make a fruity cooked syrup.

You probably have bright ideas for saving a dollar or two; list them below for easy reference. It's easy to forget good resolutions, even in cooking.

Space for writing up your own penny-pinchers:

Space for writing up your own penny-pinchers:

Recipes Using Only Egg Yolks or Egg Whites

Recipes Using Egg Yolks:

Title	No. of Yolks	Title	No. of Yolks
Onion Soup	4	Puff Paste	2
Jenny Lind's Soup	4	Orange Custard	3
Velvet Soup	3	Apricot Fool *without*	
Beer Soup	6	Meringue	4
Boudins	2	Potato Rolls	2
Mrs. Rundell's		Vanilla Sauce	4
Stuffing	2	Vanilla Ice Cream	6
Devilled Clams	2	English Ice Pudding	6
To Brown Oysters	1		
Soles	2		
Cayenne Cheese			
Straws	1		

Also: Eliza Smith's "A Fasting-Day Soup"

Recipes Using Egg Whites:

Title	No. of Whites	Title	No. of Whites
Consommé Almond	2	Almond Paste	5–6
Cheese Soufflé	3	Cream Cheese	
Fixative	1	Frosting	1
Meringue	2	Pineapple Sherbet	4
Orange Sponge	3	Chocolate Kisses	4

Also: Eliza Smith's "A Plum Cake"; and see "Half Hour Pudding"

Oven Temperature Chart
(See comments in Section I.)

Description:	In degrees:	Use for:
Slow	250° 275° 300°	Slow custards; egg, cheese dishes Milk puddings Plum cake, rich
Moderate	325° 350°	Slow roasting and baking: fish; fruit cake Moderate roasting and baking: turkey; chicken; pound cake; bread
Moderate to hot	375°	Thick cookies; short pastry
Hot	400° 425°	Quick cookies Biscuits
Very hot	450° 475°	Puff pastry Preheating

Some Useful Weights and Measures

Marion Harland and Christine
Herrick's *Modern Cooking*, 1904

"*Cup.*—A common coffee-cup is the standard. A cup of liquids is half a pint. A cupful of butter, packed solid, is 7½ ounces. A cupful of corn meal is 5 ounces. A cupful of stemmed currants, heaped up, is 6 ounces. A level cupful of flour is 4 ounces; 4 cups make 1 pound or quart. A cupful of lard is 8 ounces; 2 cupfuls of lard are 1 pound or quart. . . . A cupful of milk is 8 ounces. A cupful of molasses is 12 ounces. A cupful of oatmeal, level, is 6 ounces. A cupful of stemmed raisins is 8 ounces, or ½ pound. A cupful of granulated sugar, level, is 7 ounces. A rounded cupful is ½ pound. A cupful of brown sugar, level, is 6 ounces. A cupful of water is 8 ounces. 2 cupfuls of butter, packed solid, are 1 pound. ½ cupful of butter is ¼ pound. 3 cupfuls of corn meal are 1 pound. 2½ cupfuls of powdered sugar are 1 pound. 2 cupfuls of . . . sugar are 1 pound. 2 cups are 1 pint. 4 cups are 1 quart. 1 cup is equal to 4 wineglassfuls.

"*Tablespoon.*—14 full tablespoonfuls of liquid make 1 cup, or ½ pint. 1 tablespoonful of dry material is 3 teaspoonfuls. 4 tablespoonfuls are 1 wineglassful. 8 heaping tablespoonfuls of solids are 1 cupful. 2 rounded tablespoonfuls of flour are 1 ounce. 1 heaping tablespoonful of the spices make 1 ounce. 2 tablespoonfuls of liquid make 1 ounce. 2 rounded tablespoonfuls of coffee make 1 ounce. 2 rounded tablespoonfuls of sugar make 1 ounce. 1 large tablespoonful of butter is 2 ounces.

"*Teaspoonful.*—3 teaspoonfuls of solids make 1 tablespoonful. 4 teaspoonfuls of liquids are 1 tablespoonful. 1 heaping teaspoonful of spice is ¼ ounce. 2 rounded teaspoonfuls of mustard are ¼ ounce. 1 teaspoonful of soda is ¼ ounce. 1 teaspoonful of salt is ¼ ounce. 1 teaspoonful of pepper is ¼ ounce. 3

level teaspoonfuls of tea are ¼ ounce. 1 teaspoonful of liquid is ¼ ounce. 1 teaspoonful of liquid is 30 drops.

"4 cups of liquid make 1 quart. 2½ cups powdered sugar 1 pound, or 1 quart. 1 pint of milk or water 1 pound. 1 pint of chopped meats 1 pound. 9 large or 10 medium eggs 1 pound. 1 round tablespoonful of butter 1 ounce. 1 piece butter size of egg 1 ounce. 1 flask of olive oil 1¾ cups, or 20 tablespoonfuls. 1 small flask of Foss' Extract 12 teaspoonfuls. 1 small flask of Foss' Extract ¼ cup, or scant 3 tablespoonfuls. 1 flask of brandy 1½ cup, or 24 tablespoonfuls. 1 flask of S. M. Wine 3 cups, or 48 spoonfuls."

❧

4 gills = 1 pint = 2 cups

2 pints = 1 quart = 4 cups

2 quarts = 1 gallon = 8 cups

1 wineglass = ½ gill = ¼ cup

60 drops = 1 teaspoonful

2 teaspoonfuls liquid = 1 dessertspoon

2 dessertspoons = 1 tablespoon

3 teaspoonfuls dry = 1 tablespoon

1 saltspoonful = 1 pinch

List of Antique Cookbooks and Writers

The recipes featured are reproduced from:

title and author	first published
The Compleat Housewife or Accomplished Gentlewoman's Companion—Eliza Smith	1727
American Cookery—Amelia Simmons	1796
A New System of Domestic Management—Maria Eliza Ketelby Rundell	1806
The Indian Meal Book—Eliza Leslie	1846
Peterson's Magazine (vols. for 1 year)	1858
The Book of Household Management—Mrs. Isabella Beeton	1861
Our Digestion; or, My Jolly Friend's Secret—Dr. Dio Lewis	1872
Practical Cooking, and Dinner Giving—Mrs. Mary F. Henderson	1876
The American Housewife—Miss T. S. Shute	1879
Miss Parloa's New Cook Book—Maria Parloa	1880
La Cuisine Créole—Lafcadio Hearn	1885
The White House Cook Book—Mrs. F. L. Gillette and Hugo Ziemann	1887
Francatelli's Cook's Guide—Charles Elmé Francatelli	1888
The Table—Alessandro Filippini	1889
365 Breakfast Dishes	1901
365 Desserts	1901
Consolidated Library of Modern Cooking and Household Recipes (5 vols.)—Marion Harland and Christine Terhune Herrick	1904
The Evening Telegram Cook Book—Emma Paddock Telford	1908

Also featured:
Table Talk (Philadelphia), 1901; The Cook, circa 1890; French Cook, circa 1875
Mrs. Perry, 1824; Mrs. D. A. Lincoln, Mrs. Gesine Lemcke, both circa 1885

Except for those listed in the acknowledgments at the beginning of this book, all the recipes are taken from volumes in my private collection.

Index

Almond(s), 28, 186, 229
  Balls, 54
  Cake (Croquante), 228
  Consommé, 54
  Custard, 195
  Milk Soup, 31
  Paste, 239, 240, *241*
  Pie (à la Martha Washington), 173
  Pistachio Ice Cream, 218
Amino Acids, 28
Apple
  Cider, 259
  Custard Pie, 169
  Fritters, 255
  Pie, 167
  Pie, Plain, 168
  Preserves Fritters, 255
  Pudding, 180
  Pudding, Baked, 182
Apricot Fool, 200
Aromatic Herbaceous Seasoning, 28, 71, *260*
Arrowroot Sauce, 47, 65, 185, 195, 218, 219
Asparagus with Eggs, 140

Bacon, Sweet Potato Roulettes and, 149
Banana Ice Cream, 219
Barley Soup (Victoria), 34
Bean(s), 28, 129, 130
  Lima, 130
  Porridge, 129
  Soup, Baked, 28
  Soup, Black, 29

Beer Soup (German Method), 40
Bernhardt's Beauty Bath, 277
Bernhardt's Tonic Vinegar, 277
Bernhardt's Wrinkle Eradicator, 276
Berries. *See* individual kinds of berries
Bloaters, Potted, 263
Blueberries, 198
Blueberry (Berry) Cake, 233
Boiled Eggs, 102
Bordeaux Sauce, 77
Boudins (Chicken), 65
Brazil Nuts, 264
Bread, 247, 249–50 (*See also* Toast)
  Brown, Ice Cream, 215
  Entire or Whole Wheat, 248
  Pulled, 53, 250
  Sauce, Eggs with, 113
Brewis, 272
Broccoli with Eggs, 140
Butter Sauce, 45, 47

Cake, 225–28, 280 (*See also* Drop Cake; Shortcake)
  Berry, 233
  Cider, 233
  Croquante (Almond), 228
  Hickory, 232
  Love, 231
  Oatmeal, 252
  Plum, *236*, 239–40
  Pound, 238, 239, 240
  Rice, 230

Seed, 229
Tiered, 239–40
Wedding, 234, 235, 238
Calcium, 88, 131, 185, 264, 281
Canapés, Cheese, 119
Candied Pumpkin, 271
Cantaloupe Melons, 197
Carbohydrates, 129
Carrot Pudding, 191
Cashew Milk Soup, 31
Casseroles, 279, 280
Celery Salad, 153
Cheese, 99, 116–17, 118
Canapés, 119
Eggs Baked with, 126
Fondue, 124
Frosting, Cream, 242
Omelet, 123
Sandwiches, 127
Soufflé, 125
Straws, Cayenne, 121
Toasted, 118
Chestnut
Puree, Turkey Legs with, 72
and Tomato Soup, 30
Chicken, 58, 60, 67
Boudins, 65
Breakfast, 63
Chopped, 60
Curry (Indian Burdwan), 58
Fritters, 256
Panned, 61
Pressed, 60
Wine Croquettes, 66
Chocolate
Fig Ice Cream, 218
Ice Cream, 212
Chowder, Fish (Very Rich), 78
Christmas Pudding, 190
Chutney, Indian, 261
Cider
Apple, 259
Cake, 233
Clam(s), 80
Devilled, 80
Fritters, 256
Clay, cooking in, 82
Coconut

Cookies, 246
Ice Cream, 213, 214
Pudding, 195
Cod, 83 (See also Fish)
Balls, Dropped, 84
Gombo (Maigre), 26
Steaks à la Cardinal, 83
with Walnuts, 85
Complexion Care, 275
Consommé
Almond, 54
à l'Impératrice, 41
Cookies, 280
Coconut, 246
Crisp, 243
Ginger Snap, 245
New York, 246
Cookware, 13, 15–16
Beanpot, 130
Blender, 3
Double-boiler, 20
Ice Cream freezer, 207–9, 216
Knives, 13, 61
Omelet pan, 123
Pudding steamer, 177–78
Corn Pudding, 141
Crabs
Devilled, 81
Soft-shelled, 81
Croquettes, 64
Boudins, 65
Fruit, 64
Nut, 64, 66
Turkey, 66
Turkish, 134
Wine (Chicken), 66
Croutons, 22, 31, 51, 53
Curds, 116
Cream Cheese Frosting, 242
Cream Sauce, 44
Currants, 198
Curry
Chicken (Indian Burdwan),
58
Eggs, 112
Fowl (Indian Burdwan), 58
Indian Burdwan, 58
Indian Sauce, 43
Lamb (Indian Burdwan), 58

Powder, 43, 112, 150
Powder, American, 262
Powder, Indian, 262
Rabbit, 58
Veal, 58
Vegetable, 150
Custard, 192–93, 280
  Almond, 195
  Baked, 193
  Boiled, 193
  Orange, 193
  Pie, 193
  Pie, Apple, 169
  Pie, Dried Peach, 171
  Strawberry, 194

Dab, 92
Dandelion Salad, 153, *154*
Desserts
  Hermits, 244
  Potato Rolls, 202
  Sponge, 203
Dressing, 71 (*See also* Stuffing)
  for Fowl, 69
  Oyster, 70
  Salad, 159
Drop Cakes, Rye, 251
Drying plants, 278
Dumplings, 51

Economizing, 279–81
Economical White Sauce, 44
Egg(s), 6, 99–100, 103, 280–81,
      284 (*See also* Omelets;
      Soufflés)
  Asparagus with, 140
  Baked with Cheese, 126
  Balls, *53*, 54
  Boiled, 102
  in Boxes, 115
  in Bread Sauce, 114
  with Bread Sauce, 113
  Broccoli with, 140
  Creamed, 105
  Curried, 112
  Cutlets, 104

Dressing, Lettuce Salad with,
      157
  on Rice, 133
Eggplant Stuffed with Nuts, 142

Fat, 67, 146, 281
Fig(s), 185
  Ice Cream, Chocolate, 218
  Rice Pudding, 185
Filberts, 175
Fish, 74–75 (*See also* name of
      fish)
  Balls, 54
  Chowder (Very Rich), 78
  Cooked in Clay, 82
  Omelet, 108
  Potted, 263
  Sauce Froide, 48
  Smoked, 76
Flatulence, 180
Flounder, 92
Flour, 13, 166, 247
Flummery, 200
  Strawberry, 201
Fondue, Cheese, 124
Fool, 192, 200
  Apricot, 200
Forcemeat Balls, *41*, 51, 54
Fowl(s), 58, 67 (*See also* name
      of bird)
  Curried (Indian Burdwan),
      58
  Dressing for, 69
  Jambalaya of, and Rice, 133
Francatelli's Tomato Sauce, 43
Fritters, 254
  Apple, 255
  Apple Preserves, 255
  Chicken, 256
  Clam, 256
  French, 254
  Peach, 255
  Pineapple, 255
Frosting
  Cream Cheese, 242
  Vanilla Fudge, 242
Fruit, 13, 196 (*See also* name of
      fruit)

Croquettes, 64
Ice Cream, 214
Pulp, 281
Soup, 37
Fudge Frosting, Vanilla, 242

Garlic, 21
Ginger
Ice Cream, 218
Snaps (cookies), 245
Gombo, Shrimp or Cod (Maigre), 26
Goose, 67
Gooseberries, 49
Gooseberry Sauce
as Fish Dressing, 92
Green, 49
Grape(s), 197
Pie, 169
Gravy, Turkey, 69

Haybox, 279
Hazelnut Tarts, 175
Henbane, 259
Hermits, 244
Huckleberries with Crackers and Cream, 198
Huckleberry Shortcake, 199

Ice Cream, 207–9, 216–17
Almond/Pistachio, 218
Another Mode of, 211
Banana, 219
Brown Bread, 215
Chocolate, 212
Chocolate Fig, 218
Coconut, 213
Easy Plum Pudding, 219
Ginger, 218
Fruit, 214
Maple, 218
Nougat, 218
Peach, 218
Pure, 212
Strawberry, 219

Vanilla, 210
Wine, 218
Ice Pudding, English, 221
Indian Burdwan (Curry), 58
Iodine, 75, 88
Iron, 131, 148, 281

Jam, Strawberry, 265
Jambalaya of Fowls and Rice, 133

Lamb Curry (Indian Burdwan), 58
Lavender Scent Bag, 274
Lecithin, 281
Leftovers, 24, 28, 64, 280
Oysters, 32
Potatoes, 202
Turkey, 71
Legumes, 28
Lemon
Lettuce Salad, 156
Mint Salad, 156
Sherbet, 220
Lettuce
Lemon Salad, 156
Romaine, 154
Salad with Egg Dressing, 157
Lima Beans, 130
Lobster Sauce, 46

Mackerel, 92
Broiled Spanish, 92
with Gooseberry Sauce, 49
Magnesium, 185
Maple Ice Cream, 218
Meat, 12
Croquettes, 64
Omelet, 108
Potted, 262
Melon (See Cantaloupe)
Meringue, 196, 281
Mine Pie (Mock), 170
Minerals, 139, 150 (See also name of mineral)
Mint Lemon Salad, 156

Mushrooms, 143
  on Toast, 143

Nut(s) (*See also* name of nut)
  Butter, 264
  Croquettes, 64, 66
  Eggplant Stuffed with Nuts, 142
  and Tomato Soup, 30
Nougat Ice Cream, 218

Oatmeal, 251
  Cakes, 252
Odoriferous or Sweet-Scenting Bags, 275
Omelet(s), 106–7
  Sweet, 107
  Plain, 107
  Meat, 108
  with Fine-Herbs, 109
  Fish, 108
  Cheese, 123
  of Herbs, 109
  Rice, 134
  Rum, 111
Onion(s), 21
  Soup, 21
  Soup, French, 22
Orange
  Butter, 265
  Custard, 193
  Flower, 195
  Sauce (*See* Arrowroot Sauce)
  Sponge, 203
Oven Temperature Chart, 14, 285
Oyster(s), 32, 33, 92
  Browned in Their Own Juice, 87
  Dressing, 70
  Dressing, 70
  Shortcake, 86
  Soup, Virginia, 33

Papain, 185
Paste (*See also* Puff Paste)
  Almond, 239, 240, *241*

Short-Cake, 176
Pastry, 163–64, *166*, 169, 170, 171, 172, 174 (*See also* Puff Paste)
Peach
  Fritters, 255
  Custard Pie, Dried, 171
  Ice Cream, 218
Peanut(s), 28
  Soup, 31, 32
  and Tomato Soup, 30
Pea(s), 144
  in Potato Cases, 144
  Soup, 20
Pecans and Tomato Soup, 30
Pectin, 265
Peppers, Stuffed, 145
Perfume, 273
Phosphorus, 75, 88, 131, 141, 185, 264, 281
Pie
  Almond (à la Martha Washington), 173
  Apple, 167
  Apple Custard, 169
  Custard, 193
  Dried Peach Custard, 171
  Grape, 169
  Mock Mince, 170
  Meat, 4, 163, 164
  Plain Apple, 168
  Pumpkin, 171
  Sweet, 163–64
Pineapple
  Fritters, 255
  Sherbet, 220
Pistachio Almond Ice Cream, 218
Plum
  Cake, *236*, 239–40
  Pudding, 187, *188*
  Pudding, Christmas, 190
  Pudding Ice Cream, Easy, 219
Porridge, Bean, 129
Potassium, 23, 75, 141, 281, 185
Potato(es), 23, 144, 146, 147, 280 (*See also* Sweet Potatoes)

Baked, 146
Broiled, 147
Pancakes, 148
Cases, Peas in, 144
Rolls for Dessert, 202
Salad, 159
Soup, Irish, 23
Potato Water, 147
Pot-Pourri, 273
Potting (Meat), 262
Poultry (*See* Fowl, or name of bird)
Pressed Chicken, 60
Protein, 7, 23, 28, 33, 54, 60, 75, 99, 129, 141, 143, 144, 146, 185, 251, 264, 281
Pudding
à la Zouave, 186
Apple, 180
Baked Apple, 182
Boiled Rice, 184
Carrot, 191
Christmas Plum, 190
Coconut, 195
Corn, 141
English Ice, 221
Fig Rice, 185
Half Hour, 179
Nantucket, 253
Plum, 187, *188*
Plum, Ice Cream, 219
Quick, 183
Sweet, 177–78
Tapioca, 186
Puff Paste, *165*, 169, 170, 175
Pulled Bread, 250
Pumpkin
Candied, 271
Pie, 171
Puree, Chestnut, with Turkey Legs, 72

Rabbit Curry (Indian Burdwan), 58
Raisins, 186
Raspberry Sherbet, 221

Rice, 13, 131–32
Cake, 230
Eggs on, 133
Fig (Pudding), 185
Jambalaya of Fowls and, 133
Omelet, 134
Pudding, Boiled, 184
Soup (Victoria), 34
Waffles, 251
Rose Water, 195
Rum Omelet, 111
Rye, 251

Sauces, 42–43, 45
Arrowroot, *47*, 65, 185, 195, 218, 219
Bordeaux, 77
Butter, *45*, 47
Bread, 113
Fish (Froide), 48
Green Gooseberry, 49
Indian, 43
Lobster, 46
Shrimp, 46
Strawberry, 219
Tomato (Francatelli's), 43
Tomato (Indian), 43
Vanilla, 202
White, 45
White (Economical), 44
Sago Soup
Hawaiian Recipe, 39
Jenny Lind's, 35
Velvet, 36
Salads, 151–52, 153, 155
Celery, 153
Dandelion, 153, *154*
English, 154, 155
Japanese, 158
Lettuce Lemon, 156
Lettuce with Egg Dressing, 157
Mint Lemon, 156
Potato, 159
Salad Dressing, 159
Salmon, 88
Broiled (Smoked), 88
Fillets of, à la Indienne, 89

Sandwiches, Cheese, 127
Sardines, 90, 95
  Sauté, 90
Scallops, 90
  Baked, 91
  Fried, 91
Scent Powder, 272
Seed Cake, 229
Seeds (*See* names of seeds)
Seasoning, Aromatic Herbace-
  ous, 28, 71, *260*
Sesame Seeds, 28
Shortcake
  Huckleberry, 199
  Oyster, 86
  Paste, 176
  Strawberry, 199
Sherbet
  Lemon, 220
  Pineapple, 220
  Raspberry, 221
Shrimp
  Gombo (Maigre), 26
  Sauce, 46
Smoked Fish, 76
Sodium, 75
Sole, 92
  Fried, 93
  Pie, 94
Soufflé(s), 101
  Cheese, 125
Soup(s), 19–20, 51
  Almond, Milk, 31
  Baked Bean, 28
  Barley (Victoria), 34
  Beer (German Method), 40
  Black Bean, 29
  Cashew Milk, 31
  Consommé à l'Impératrice, 41
  French Onion, 22
  Fruit, 37
  Herb with Parmesan, 25
  Irish Potato, 23
  Jenny Lind's, 35
  Nut and Tomato, 30
  Onion, 21
  Pea, 20
  Peanut, 31, *32*
  Rice (Victoria), 34

Sago (Hawaiian Recipe), 39
Sago (Jenny Lind's), 35
Sago (Velvet), 36
Squash, 24
Tapioca (Velvet), 36
Turnip, 24
Velvet, 36
Virginia Oyster, 33
Victoria, 34
Sour Cream (with Meat
  Dishes), 62
Soybeans, 129
Squash Soup, 24
Strawberries, 194, *197*
Strawberry
  Custard, 194
  Flummery, 201
  Ice Cream, 219
  Jam, 265
  Sauce, 219
  Shortcake, 199
Stuffing, 71 (*See also* Dressing)
  for Fowl, 69
  Mrs. Rundell's, 77
  Oyster, 70
Sugar, 12, 13
Sulphur Acids, 75, 141, 281
Sunflower Seeds, 28
Sweet Potato(es), 148, 149
  Roulettes and Bacon, 149
Syllabubs, 200

Tapioca
  Pudding, 184, *186*
  Soup (Velvet), 36
Tarts, 163, 164, 175
  Hazelnut, 175
Toast
  Buttered, 250
  Mushrooms on, 143
Tomato and Nut Soup, 30
Tomato Sauce, 105, 110, 145
  Francatelli's, 43
  Indian, 43
Trifles, 244
Turkey, 57–58, 67
  Croquettes, 66
  Gravy, 69

Legs with Chestnut Puree, 72
Roast, 68
Scallop, 71
Stew, 57
Turkish Croquettes, 134
Turnip Soup, 24

Vanilla
Ice Cream, 210
Sugar, 203
Sauce, 202
Veal Curry (Indian Burdwan),
58
Vegetable(s), 3, 7, 13, 139–40,
152, 191 (*See also* name of
vegetable)
Curry, 150
Vinegar, Bernhardt's Tonic, 277
Vitamin(s), 20, 130, 131, 139,
141, 147, 150, 153
A, 23, 281
B, 23, 148, 281
C, 23, 53, 144, 148, 194

Waffles, Rice, 251
Walnuts, Codfish with, 85
Weights and Measures, 286–87
Welsh Rarebit, 119, *120*
au Gratin, 120
with Poached Egg (Golden
Buck), 121
Whey, 116, 117
Whitebait, Devilled, 95
White Fish
Baked (Bordeaux Sauce), 77
Boiled, 76
Wine, 163
Croquettes (Chicken), 66
Ice Cream, 218
Wrinkle Eradicator, Bernhardt's,
276

Yeast, 249–50
Yogurt, 198
with Meat Dishes, 62